THE PRAIRIE
IN HER EYES

THE PRAIRIE
IN HER EYES

ANN DAUM

MILKWEED EDITIONS

Published by Milkweed Editions
Printed in the United States of America
Jacket and interior design by Dale Cooney
Jacket photo by Ann Daum
Author photo by Mark Kayser
Photo on back cover courtesy of the author
Photo on p. ii by Brenda Daum
The text of this book is set in Legacy Serif.
03 04 05 06 23 22 21 20

"Coyote" and "Calving Heifers in a March Blizzard" (a section in "What We Lose") were first
published in *Intimate Nature: The Bond between Women and Animals,* edited by Linda Hogan,
Deena Metzger, and Brenda Peterson (New York: Ballantine, 1998).

Milkweed Editions, a nonprofit publisher, gratefully acknowledges support from our
World As Home funders: Lila Wallace-Reader's Digest Fund; and Reader's Legacy under-
writer Elly Sturgis. Other support has been provided by the Elmer L. and Eleanor J. Andersen
Foundation; Bush Foundation; Faegre and Benson Foundation; General Mills Foundation;
Jerome Foundation; Marshall Field's Project Imagine with support from the Target Foundation
and Target Stores; McKnight Foundation; Minnesota State Arts Board through an appropria-
tion by the Minnesota State Legislature and a grant from the National Endowment for the
Arts; Norwest Foundation on behalf of Norwest Bank Minnesota; Lawrence and Elizabeth
Ann O'Shaughnessy Charitable Income Trust in honor of Lawrence M. O'Shaughnessy;
Oswald Family Foundation; Ritz Foundation on behalf of Mr. and Mrs. E. J. Phelps Jr.; John
and Beverly Rollwagen Fund of the Minneapolis Foundation; St. Paul Companies, Inc.; U.S.
Bancorp Foundation; and generous individuals.

Library of Congress Cataloging-in-Publication Data

Dautn, Ann, 1970-
    The Prairie in her eyes / Ann Daum.
      p. cm.
    ISBN r-57131-255-2 (cloth)
      I. Daum, Ann, 1970- 2. Women ranchers-South Dakota-Biography. 3. Ranch life-
    South Dakota. 4. South Dakota-Social life and customs. 5. South Dakota-
    Description and travel. 6. Prairies-South Dakota. 7. Natural history-South Dakota.
    8. Landscape-South Dakota. 9. White River Region (S.D.)-Biography. ro. White River
    Region (S.D,)-Description and travel. I. Title.

F656-4.D38 A3 2001
978.3' 63-dc2r
[BJ

2ooro18673

For my father,
Johnny G. Daum,
the storyteller

THE PRAIRIE IN HER EYES

*Thanks to my family, for believing in me always,
and to everyone who helped along the way.*

THE PRAIRIE
IN HER EYES

THE HABIT OF RETURN

Last night I was wakened by the voices of sandhill cranes. The sound came through the glass of my window and woke me slowly, into another kind of dream. A flock of cranes makes a rippling kind of music, like the echo of an echo, a fluttering and tapering off to silence. There is no other sound like it. I sat up slowly and looked outside.

At first I saw only stars and the moon's pale glow rising from the east. I looked at the clock—nine o'clock. I must have just fallen asleep. I thought I saw shadows moving outside the window, against the moonlight, but I wasn't sure. I'd never heard of sandhill cranes flying by night. I crept outside in my nightclothes, barefoot onto a dew so cold it burned my feet. The sky was a whirlpool of cranes, their voices coming from all around. I stood in the center of it, looking up. I remember thinking that if the stars had voices they might sing like this.

I stood there until the last unseen crane had passed, intent on her invisible arc from spring resting grounds in

Nebraska to nesting sites farther north. The voices lingered in the darkness, coming from all directions and none, before fading away. The frost had melted under my feet; I traced my footprints back into the house.

Sandhill cranes keep returning to find home roosts plowed under or slathered with concrete—their home is shrinking. They have had to adjust more in the last hundred years than in the millions since the Pliocene when they evolved.

The cranes now roost on only a tiny stretch of their former habitat along Nebraska's North Platte River. Water needed to keep the Platte's channel wide and clear enough for cranes has been diverted for other uses. Meadows needed by the cranes for their macroinvertebrate life—their snails and earthworms and insects—are being plowed under or developed. And while new stretches of cornfields are providing cranes with previously undreamed of sources of energy, corn can't replace the protein and calcium found in the native grassy soil.

Cranes now spend equal portions of their day foraging for the 3 percent of their diet formed by macroinvertebrates as they do seeking the 97 percent of their diet made up of corn. They roost and forage wing to wing, crowded in their shrinking world.

For the better part of the past ten years I have been moving between school, work, and travel—arriving home to my family's South Dakota ranch in time for foaling and calving season in the spring and leaving after harvest in the fall. And every year, like the birds, I see the places I know and that I call home changing and shrinking and crumbling away.

When I was a little girl, my father ran cattle and farmed on 30,000 acres owned in a partnership with his brothers Ned and Pete. In the late eighties, the partnership split up, leaving my family with 13,000 acres, my childhood universe. Now that universe has shrunk again. We have managed to hold on to only 4,000 of those acres, and almost all of them are leased out to a neighbor now. My parents are retired, and I live together with them in our ranch house by the river. From the living-room window we can now see across to land owned by someone else. We have kept 130 acres out of the lease for me and my twenty horses. It doesn't seem like much compared to what we had, but it is enough.

This losing of a ranch is considered a kind of shame. All over South Dakota, farmers and ranchers are going out of business and running out of hope. I've heard the story before. But living it hurts. Talking about the loss doesn't seem to do much good. These days, when my cousins talk about the wind and weather, wheat and cattle prices, they look at the toes of their boots or out the window. I want to look away.

~ ~ ~

Two days later, on the first of April, cranes fill the sky— hundreds, thousands, all flying north in billowing, V-shaped threads. I stand outside and look up. Sometimes the threads weave together and the whole skyful of cranes comes together and begins to circle. They float like leaves in a dust devil—a funnel of birds reaching halfway across the sky. The sky here is not too wide for so many cranes.

All day they pass over the White River valley. They speak to each other constantly in flight, so that a passing flock of sandhill cranes sounds like distant singing—a chorus sung in rounds, again and again. While I am standing, looking up, one crane passes lower than the rest, at about the height of the top branches of a cottonwood tree. I can see the patch of red on his crest, the spear-shaped beak and narrow, silver neck. He sees me, too, and I imagine he wishes he were higher up.

When I drive to Okaton to get my mail, I keep scanning the sky for cranes. I don't see any from the topland. I drive back a little faster than I should. Storm clouds are piling in the south and east, and as I drop into the valley, the sun highlights another moving string of cranes.

There will be snow tonight, and the wind is beginning to blow, flattening the yellow stems of last year's grasses. Snow in western South Dakota blows sideways into hard, no-color drifts. I wonder, sometimes, why the birds bother coming back this way at all. But birds are stubborn, like the people here. They have the habit of return, I suppose, but the habit seems a little bit like love. They keep coming back.

WHAT'S LEFT

I wanted to look away, but my job was counting cows. Charlie,
the brand inspector, stood by the gate. I sat up on a post.
We compared numbers every twenty head or so. The cows
went out of the corrals in clumps, none wanting to lead a
group, none wanting to gallop through alone. That instinct
made counting difficult, like trying to pick flies out of a
swarm with your forefinger and thumb. You learn not to
focus on any one cow too long or you'll lose count. The
count is all that matters. After a while, the cows all look
the same, blur into something not quite real that can be
counted and sold. You don't really have to see them go.

No one said much after the count was finished. The guys
joked and snapped their ropes at dogs and fence posts. A
few Styrofoam cups had blown out of the back of my pickup
and I chased them down to where they caught on grasses.
Charlie took a long time writing up the bill of sale. He was
a big man and out of breath by the time he straightened up
and handed me his pen. I, the rancher's daughter, would

sign away the cattle. It wasn't a job I wanted, but my father was home sitting in his wheelchair, his fingers too clumsy and stiff from his diabetes to sign his name.

"Sure we got 'em all?" Charlie asked. "Once we sign, it's official." I shrugged. We'd started riding at dawn—Pres on his liver chestnut stallion, Pres's son, Stan, and three hired men all riding big, rangy bays that could cover ground. I rode TJ, my blaze-faced sorrel gelding, and found myself remembering at odd moments—crossing the dam grade, our reflection hazy against the gathering shadows of morning clouds; galloping down a hill after a bucking, red, brockle-faced calf—that this would be our last roundup together. I rode alone most of the morning, seeking out the farthest corners of the pasture. If there were any more of my father's cattle out there they must be in a neighbor's pasture.

"I think that's all of them, Charlie," I said.

Pres cleared his throat. "Came up short on heifers," he added. As the buyer, it wasn't Pres's job to point out shortages, but he is honest, as ranchers tend to be out here. Since he's leasing my father's land as well as buying our cattle, it pays to be a good neighbor. He took off his dusty cowboy hat and ran one hand through his short, gray hair. "But we didn't leave anything out there. Must have counted a few in with the dry cows."

"Don't matter," Charlie said after a pause. "You're getting the same price for dry cows and first-calf heifers, right? We're set to go, Annie. You sign here."

I nodded. The paper fluttered on the hood of the truck; the pen shook in my hand.

You want to look away. From anything that's hard and

not changing and that you don't want to be that way. Signing a paper is admitting you're giving up. Writing about it afterward is like looking into the sun, or standing out in an open field, watching a tornado sweep toward you. You want to be inside, covering your eyes. Every instinct says, don't look, don't say it, and it might not come true.

So I look. It is like looking at the sun. There's a blank spot in the heart of things, bright and burning. I blink, but there are blind spots. I see the edges and work my way inside.

"Take good care of them," I said to Pres. And I signed the paper.

Afterward I lay in the grass downslope of the corrals. There had been rain in August so the wheat grass hid me, or I imagined it so. I could see straight up into wind-polished sky. Cows were still bawling for their calves down by the dam, though they'd been pairing up now for just over an hour.

After a little while I stood up. My horse had worked himself loose and was pushing his nose against the rails, lipping at some grass outside the panels.

The corrals hadn't been used since June branding—they'd grown perfect meadows of crested wheat grass and sweet yellow clover during this long summer of little use. Now they were back to black ovals of hoof-pitted gumbo. I find it strange how small empty corrals can seem. Who ever knows what kind of space five hundred cows will leave behind?

What's left are horses. Eight mares heavy with foal, six yearlings, two two-year-olds, and an assortment of green-broke three- and four-year-olds. Twenty-three in all, counting the three ranch horses we're feeding for no better reason than because it's hard to see them go. Kind of silly now that we've sold the cattle. But there they are—two grays and a sorrel, winter coats unmarked by sweat or saddle galls though it's calving season, muzzles pushed deep inside the round bale feeder.

I count off on my calendar the mornings left until my eight mares foal. They are my future, and my father has joined me in making these coming foals into the stuff of hopes and dreams. He talks of little else when he calls me from his winter home in south Texas. Doesn't mention the cattle we've sold or land we've leased. He asks me how the mares are.

What's also left are the land and the stories of my family. Four thousand acres may be leased out to a neighbor, but they still feel like my home. The land holds me here; I keep returning. My family's stories have soaked into this ground, like blood. They tingle up through the soles of my feet, like lightning choosing a pathway from ground to sky, choosing the same hill, the same tree, time after time. The stories whisper up through stems of grass and look at me from faces in the clouds.

What's left for me is to put them back together—my family and the land, my stories and my father's, the horses, the past and present and future. To stare headlong into the sun and start to see again.

SILENCE AND SPACES

Rain never falls in the South Dakota of my childhood. Wind blows down the valley with the force of locomotives, clouds pile on the horizon, thunder growls from the west. Once, sometimes twice, a summer, lightning sparks prairie fires that crackle and spit, swallow brown summer grasses without tasting. The flames cough embers up like glowing stars and the smoke hangs in clouds. But there is no rain.

The pictures in our family album are full of sky and golden dust instead of grass. Miles of dry, empty space stretch beyond the white Polaroid frames.

We are smiling in those photos, squinting into the blazing sun in our Sunday clothes. There are five of us: mother smiling shyly, not showing her crooked teeth; father, sunburned and stout with ranching muscle, standing with one leg cocked and both hands curled uneasily into his brown, western suit pants; sister Brenda, blond and smiling, proud to bare her small, even white teeth; brother David, all elbows and knees, with lengths of bare wrist and ankle in last year's blue suit. I am bare legged, shoeless, sockless in most of these pictures. Freckled and sunburned, standing apart from the rest. I am thin, dry boned as a sparrow, so that the wind might blow right through me, never making a sound.

I learned about silence from the land, and from a father who loved to talk. I heard his stories so many times I knew them by heart—I was the listener, there on his knee, or beside him on the bench seat of a pickup. It became a habit, I suppose, so that I learned to take things in. Later, when I had stories of my own to tell, I rode out to check cows, where there were no voices, only the sound of the wind and the grasses answering back. I whispered my secrets into this wind, and watched them blow away.

I loved the land and my family in much the same way. And yet I dreamed at night of a place all my own, where lightning never stabbed the cattle on the hills, where rain fell soft as dew on rolling hills of grass. And I drew all the vast emptiness of the dry, rolling prairie with its bristle-toothed yuccas and long, lonesome hills into my heart.

My sister told me when I was fifteen about my brother Paul, born three years before me. He lived just four days, his lungs wet and fragile as old lace. I wonder if my mother mourned him while she was pregnant with me; I imagine her sitting in the old wooden rocking chair by the cold living-room window for hours at a time, never rocking.

There is so much I don't know, buried beneath my family's reluctance to talk of painful things. Why there is only one picture of me as a baby in the fat family albums. Why my parents never told me about my first tooth, or the way I cried when the pastor baptized me. Why they don't remember my first word. When I ask, my mother seems flustered. Wrinkles bunch on her forehead, her eyes soften and dim. She can't remember.

I stare at the one picture I can find of myself as a baby, trying to understand. I am perched in a high chair, alone outside on the darkening lawn except for a yellow tomcat winding around the four stilty legs of the chair. I am smiling, simple and flushed in a red striped dress and white lace bonnet, reaching with one fat, open hand for something outside the picture. Behind me the cornfield stretches pale and thirsty green, and a great, leaden cloud casts its shade over the chair, over the cat, over me. The air of the photograph seems charged, as if lightning may strike at any time, and there I am: dry, happy, ignorant. It tells me nothing.

I try to pull memories from that place they're buried and make some sense of them. There are so many things I can only imagine.

Like my parents' seventy-mile drive home from the hospital the year Paul was born. A spring storm dumping six inches of snow on western South Dakota; ice coats the roads, the humped-up backs of cattle, everything. My parents driving the long slick road from Pierre with a child-sized box in the backseat. My mother crying, steaming her pearl-wing glasses, leaning against the cold passenger window of the four-door LTD. She's wearing a wrinkled maternity dress under her brown felt coat, her hands twisted in knots in her lap, her soft, dark hair pulled back from her face with bobby pins. Her forehead is white, the skin stretched paper-thin to crinkle at the corners of her eyes.

She's trying not to look at the box in the backseat and that means looking everywhere else, at the dull brown-ice South Dakota prairie, at the dull blue sky, at the dull slushy highway stretching forever in front of her and the box. She is trying so hard not to remember.

My father drives one-handed, the other fiddles with the hem of my mother's coat. Just last week he'd promised to teach the baby, the third, the last, to drive the new Deutz-Allis tractor. "Boy or girl, it doesn't matter to me!" he sang through the house to the tune of "Oklahoma," my mother laughing along, swollen feet perched on the brown-patterned couch. David, old enough to laugh along, too, shouts "Brother!" when asked what he'd get for his birthday. Brenda, spitting slobber in her fist, white haired as an angel, laughs because everyone is laughing and planning and tasting this new baby already, like a fruitcake opened early. I can picture this.

My parents stop along old Highway 16 between Vivian and Draper, on the swell of a lonely prairie hill, out of sight of any ranch houses. It is a place where the dry grass whispers up against the car and the snow's so white, no one's ever been. This seems like a place to say good-bye: the last place, the last time, this baby will be truly theirs—no funeral director yet; no coffin. They hold the box carefully between them. Brenda told me this part, about stopping the car on the roadside, holding the box for one last good-bye before leaving Paul in Murdo, at the funeral home, so I know it's true. I can see it so clearly. "Don't drop him, Johnny," my mother saying, then silent again. Tears run in tiny chasms, splitting, branching from the corners of her eyes like rivers. Exactly like rivers.

She is still crying thirty-nine months later when they bring me home. This time in the breathing-out of August 1970, in the middle of a tight, dry heat that scorched like an open oven door. They say the summer I was born was the hottest in years. A parching of wheat fields and men's mouths blown to dust in their sleep. I imagine my mother's crying. It was the only wet the wide, dry sky offered me.

I grew up in a seven-year string of droughts, remember crackling grasshoppers under every step of my brown suede church shoes. Dust sat like fog in the folds and creases of our valley, hid the chokecherry brambles down by the cane field, the hollow cottonwood forests farther to the west, even the mountainous silver silos just down the road from our house. The wide White River dried down to a silty stream those summers, refused to feed the parched gray earth. Just wound and coiled through the valley like a slackened rope, reflecting back storm clouds on the clearest days.

Plowed fields blew down Highway 83, south into Nebraska, and some of the farmers followed. Vanderwalls, Beckwiths, Oldenkamps, my father's younger brother Nick, all packed up their families and moved south, into Nebraska, Kansas, Colorado. . . . Others didn't stop till they reached California. Most of them never came back, even to visit.

The farmers who stayed were worried men with wind-cracked hands and red skin around the borders of their caps. The women wore cotton dresses with belts and thick, brown panty hose all day long. They hung plastic bread bags on the line to dry and use again. Children wore their older brothers' shoes to class, helped with chores as soon as they could wear rubber boots, carried buckets of scraps out for the chickens.

I think the drought shaped me as the White River did our valley. Spaces grew inside that had nothing to do with how well my mother fed me, how many stories my father told. Spaces that had nothing at all to do with the joy I was supposed to feel if I let Jesus step inside me in the chilly basement of our church. How could I explain that God was in the open sky and the brittle winter humming of the grass? How could I tell my Sunday school teacher, dim-eyed Eva Baughman with her gray hair clenched inside a hand-crocheted net, that I felt nothing when we prayed? Nothing and nothing and nothing.

In family photos, David and Brenda are larger than I am—stronger, browner, braver kids. They tanned in the same sun and wind that burned my freckles raw, seemed to know everything I didn't about barn-sour horses and pickups that wouldn't start. As a child I was scared of vacuum cleaners, afraid to gallop down hills, flush toilets in strange bathrooms, and plug Christmas-tree lights into outlets. Inside Polaroid frames, I am puny and unsure—almost invisible.

What's funny is, I'm the only one who's stayed. David

is a computer programmer, living in Indonesia with his wife and kids. Brenda is a doctor living in Dallas. She, at least, comes back to the ranch every couple of months. She loves the horses and the rolling hills almost as much as I do, but she's found out she's happier living somewhere else. People can lose themselves in the spaces here.

If there is anyone in my family who knows about spaces, it is my mother. She moved, like so many prairie women, from a greener, more densely peopled place. She grew up in a lake town in Minnesota, surrounded by trees and the kind of green only water and cultivation bring. The prairie has been hard on her. Ladies here don't meet often just out of friendship. There's Bible study and ladies aid, church suppers and prayer meetings. But few friends to gossip with on the phone.

Her gardens, the neat rows of potatoes, beans, and tomatoes, the hills of watermelon and squash creeping toward the sweet corn, took up nearly a quarter acre of land. My father cheerfully plowed a space for her garden each spring, and Brenda and I helped drop seeds into the furrows she hoed. Every June she wore a floppy hat and gloves outside to work amidst the sturdy green and brown of her cultivated rows. And every August, drought would take it all back—bake the soil to cracking, brown cement, bring grasshoppers and potato bugs to gnaw her precious plants to leafless stalks. By fall, weeds stood in great shaggy rings around the garden's border, taller than any other plant.

There are few photos of my mother taken when I was growing up, as if her place in the family wasn't quite as important as ours. Though of course it was. My mother was the steady one, quiet, always there. She roasted thick cuts of beef, basted them brown all afternoon, then boiled vegetables and baked apple crisps for our supper. She bought books and encyclopedias and *National Geographic* magazines and opened up my world. She patched my baggy jeans with hearts stitched from red calico, pushed cat-eye glasses up her nose a thousand times and fed me butterscotch-chip treasure bars after school.

She loved me in a quiet way, not buying little presents or teasing as my father would. Rarely criticizing either. But when she spoke my name I'd always look up, blank for a second, as if she were calling someone else. Some other child not quite there. I saw him in her veiled brown eyes, felt him through her soap-wrinkled fingertips even before I knew his name. Long before I knew his name.

I don't mean to say my mother ignored me, didn't love me. She was wholly unselfish in her love. I mean that I didn't really know her, never realized she might be lonely. Those secrets and hidden pain kept us apart as surely as the forty-years' age difference between us. I'm not sure I even knew my mother's given name, Jane Louise, back then, when I was six, even seven or eight years old, yet I knew the name of every draw and ridge in the north pasture, the precise shade of gray a thundercloud shimmered the instant before a rain.

My father is the storyteller of the family. In a land of few words, my father is rarely silent. Maybe he's had enough of that just living on the plains; wants to fill the space around him with something more.

From the time I was up to his knee I remember him filling whole houses with his belly-deep laugh, crouched scowling in the corner to act out a badger's role in a story he was telling. Always proud of the ranch and his herd of cows, he loved equally having houseguests and telling stories. The two, of course, went hand in hand.

I suspect our houseguests never forgot my father. He glowed and came alive around people, and animals, too. I've heard him telling stories to the ranch dogs, talking to geese and waiting for them to answer back. Always a trickster, he liked to scare guests by driving his Ford pickup down the steepest prairie draws—so steep we all hit our heads on the roof when we surfaced on the other side.

"That was nothing," he'd say, gleeful, and aim for a knot of cows standing on the farthest hillside. The guests held on to the dashboard, door handles, each other.

You'd think he'd be solemn, growing up in the thirties' dust bowl as he did. His father died young of encephalitis, or "sleeping sickness," leaving ten children and a wife whose bouts of "quietness" would be called depression in today's world. But hardship marked him in the way heat will sometimes sweeten fruit—he sees few problems that can't be solved, somehow. Even now, with the cattle sold, he believes we can hang on—at least to what's left of our land—and perhaps build up the herd again. He sees the horses, and my breeding operation, as a source of hope. For my father, there is nothing that can't be done through hard work and dreams, in equal parts.

When I ask about life in the thirties—the drought and grasshoppers eating paint from houses—he tells instead of workhorses he rode bareback across fields or the time he tied strings to his sisters' boots, hid beneath the stairs, and yanked the strings in the middle of the night so the girls would think a ghost was walking across their bedroom floor.

As a boy my father used to trap skunks and sell their skins—it was one way a schoolboy could make money back then. When turkey hunters stop by for coffee, he likes to talk about those days. I think they are clearer to him than the present, and certainly more fun to talk about.

"I couldn't smell it but the teacher sure did," my father begins. "Old John P. Andrews turned around and looked at us all, kind of suspicious. He had eyes like buckshot—little, hard, and black. 'Who smells like skunk?' he said."

His eyes stopped on my dad. "It's *you*, Johnny. Go home and change your clothes." So my father did, and then returned.

The teacher stood at the blackboard for a long moment, and my father swears he could see his nose twitch, like a skunk's. He shows us, his face bunched up as if behind a set of whiskers.

"*Johnny!*" the teacher thundered. "You still stink!"

My father looked down, thought awhile. "It's my shoes," he said. "That skunk was aiming pretty low."

The rest of the class laughed, but the teacher sent him

home again. "You don't come back until you no longer smell of *skunk*."

This time my father thought about the problem awhile. This was his only pair of shoes.

"I figured it out just fine," he says, voice sinking to a whisper. "I found a can of *turpentine!*"

So my father returned to school proud—his shoes freshly painted with turpentine, no longer smelling of skunk. When the teacher sent him home again, he told my father not to come back until his shoes smelled like shoes.

"And *that* was quite some time!" he says, laughing.

When he's telling stories, my father can almost fill a room. He's not a tall man, but he is rather stout, in the way of cottonwood branches or Angus bulls. And to tell the truth, he is not stout in this way anymore—his diabetes has taken the strength out of him, leaving behind an old man who has lost a leg and struggles to maneuver his canes over ruts in the gravel road. But when he tells his stories, it is easy to believe that his two legs are whole again and his thick hands can carry salt blocks and wrestle tractor tires, hold tight the ranch with all its life and worries and fragrant hope.

My father begins his stories with the same eagerness, the same trembling energy of a rope horse waiting to charge out of the box. He leans forward, eyes gleaming, hands curling and uncurling in his lap. He drops his voice down to a whisper, knows just when to raise it, knows how to make the world come alive with his words.

In the past my sister and I conspired to protect his audience. We'd heard the stories before—many times before—and if the visitor seemed edgy after the first hour, stealing glances at the door or at his watch, we stepped in to remark on the weather for driving or perhaps the lateness of the day. We touched my father's sleeve, saying tactfully that he'd talked too long, or perhaps this person had heard enough about animal telepathy and UFOs.

I'd like to say that I've always been proud of my father, of his creative energy, his raw enthusiasm for making life into one tremendous story. But for years I was embarrassed. I would look at the floor and mumble, "That's not how it is," when he told of my genius with horses or ability to foretell the future through my dreams. I'd wilt into the couch as he told my college friends about his skunk-trapping days, or some prize I'd won in high school that I'd forgotten and he remembered as the award given to the valedictorian of the class, which I wasn't. There wasn't any use arguing. He'd remember it the same way the next time. But I looked down at the floor, ears red to the skull, wishing I had never been born, at least to this father, who grew up during the depression in a tiny house with no electricity and nine brothers and sisters. Who put together a kaleidoscope of land and family and story and knew how to be proud of it all.

Memories of my father seem tied up with the excess of lightning and wind and storms. In one of my earliest memories we are standing in the front yard, his face a blur above my fist-hold of brown denim, and the rest is sky. I pull on his pant leg, and he picks me up but never looks at me. I know this is my father by the sand of his whiskers, the sharp smell of silage and old sweat, the excitement I feel but can't see in his eyes. He's looking straight up, into the hot of the sky, not at me. I look up, too, and the sky rolls down to meet me, gray and black and so close I smell the coming rain like breath. When the clouds split open, I scream with the crash of light and endless roar of thunder.

He made me notice storms, and his obsession with them soured in me to fear. I remember my terror of lightning; the rare storm dwindling to water spinning off the crooked eaves outside my window, pooling dark and still beneath the drooping apple tree; hail pellets shattering like mirrors on the cement steps.

I learned from him that the silent strength of jet streams ruled our lives. He stood on the porch, sweeping his great, muscled arms from west to east to show how warm air mixes with the cool. I knew how fronts rolled in from the time I could say my ABCs, knew about thunderheads boiling black and gray just outside my bedroom window, then passing by without loosing a drop. I pictured the jet stream as a mighty river of air, thundering above our heads. Some days high, feather-white cirrus tumbled down invisible currents of air. Other days the jet stream seemed a languid blue river dotted with low, lazy cumulus clouds poling their way east, one Huck Finn, one the magnificent face of an angel. Stratus clouds alone seemed to defy that river of air. They stretched as far east as the horizon, heavy, gray, oblivious—like tissue paper settling face down just above our heads.

The whole summer I was nine my father waited for a hailstorm, fingering every thunderbolt, every greenish gray cloud, waiting. Loving and dreading and waiting. Finally, in the midst of all that drought, it came.

"Get the car in, Mother!" he bellowed through the screen door one broiling July afternoon. His face red, sweat running into the collar of his long-sleeved snap-up shirt, and talking so fast his words bled into each other. "This is a big one, girls! Get that garden covered! Get the car inside, Mother! There's hail in this one!" And he was gone, running to park the rest of the vehicles inside.

My mother dropped her dishcloth, ran to start the big gold Mercury. Brenda pulled open the cupboard below the sink, disappeared to the tip of her long, blond ponytail, then came out with a stack of plastic ice-cream buckets.

"Help me cover the tomatoes," she ordered, but I was already out the door and catching cats. Kelly the calico, old yellow BunBine, Peaches and her kitten, Cream, all stuffed in the garage, door slammed on their yowling faces. All except Angel, my favorite kitty, black with an orange halo covering her face. I ran all the way past the silos calling her. "Keeeeety, Keeeeeety, Kitty-Kitty-Kitty!" Barely noticed the sun going out like a pinched candle, the first heavy drops of rain stabbing through my cotton shirt.

I was still searching through the yellow kochia weeds along the granary when Dad pounded up behind me, grabbed my arm, and pulled me back along the gravel road toward the house. Wind hit and ripped away the words I saw him yelling just inches from my ear. Then hailstones dropped with the suddenness and speed of baseballs and we were safe in the garage and I was shaking, covering my ears against the terrible noise.

I'd never seen hail so big, coming down so thick I couldn't see across the driveway. I wanted Angel, wondered if this might be the judgment Pastor Waley preached from Revelation, the storm my Sunday school book showed crushing sinners under balls of ice big as cars. Pictured Angel crushed and bleeding. I think I cried.

My father didn't say anything else. He didn't even look at me again until the hail had turned to thick, white sheets of rain. He stood at the open door and watched, hands hanging dumbly by his belt. Watched the cane field in front of the barn stripped to bleeding green stalks, watched a river form and fork and split from the ditch along the road.

I looked up at him when it was over, when the piles of ice on the concrete outside began to steam and melt and the rain turned soft as a dripping faucet. His broad face was white, the excitement drained away and nothing left to replace it. Nothing at all. Just silence and the wheat fields in his eyes, stems broken and scattered like driftwood.

Then he was angry with me, and his face flushed back to red.

"You don't worry about cats in a storm like that," he shouted, then leaned over and shook me. Not hard, but his fingers felt like steel. "You gotta get some sense, girl!" He didn't even look at me when he was saying this, his eyes hard and mean on some far-off place.

"Cats live anywhere. They always find some place to go.

People get swept away in storms like that, but never cats. Never blasted cats."

This look he gave me then, this loving, hating, knowing look is maybe what I remember most of all about my father. It was a look that hid behind his laughter sometimes. A look that knew about storms and about lives swept away by waters outside any human control.

That look was the story I heard all through my life, maybe never really believed until that day of the hail. The one about a cloudburst in 1932 that killed Dad's brother Nickie.

The older boys in the Nicholas Daum family were supposed to bring the cows in each afternoon from the hilly south pasture. Ned, six, and Pete, five, started earlier than usual that morning, stopped to play in the fallow fields stretching empty and weed-blown along the dirt road leading to town. Four-year-old Nickie had followed the bigger boys, eager to help. Nickie refused to go back to the house, carried the dried spear of a ragweed into the field, whacking at the rocks and clods of dirt as he walked. Pete shrugged, rolled his eyes at tall, lanky Ned, and ignored the little boy. Around noon Bertha Oldenkamp walked by, saw the boys playing among last year's broken stems and stalks of wheat, and stopped to warn them. Black clouds were lining up in the west, and the wind was blowing those weeds and dry stalks of wheat almost flat to the ground. Bertha yelled that the boys had better hurry, get the cattle in before the storm hit. Pete and Ned took one look at the sky, at the coming of night in the middle of day, and started running south. Nickie clumped along, still swinging his ragweed sword.

My dad was three years old, too young to follow, and so he lived.

The storm that blew across the prairie from the west that day has not been equaled since. Twelve inches of rain in under half an hour. Hail big as half-grown melons, water running down the draws like mighty rivers.

The boys never reached the cattle. Ned crawled to the top of a hill, sat shivering through the rain and hail, waiting. Pete tumbled with the water down a draw, caught a strand of barbed-wire fence and held on with bleeding palms until his father found him, hauled him from the sucking water. Pete had held on, thinking all the time that Nickie was right behind him, or just a little down the draw. But Nickie wasn't there. He had floated through the space between the barbed-wire strands, down the roaring draw, and out of sight. A hundred men searched for his body in the next six days and never found a shoe or hat or bone. My Uncle Pete thinks Nickie floated all the way to the river valley, seven miles below. Somewhere, where those flood waters met the White River, he is buried still.

The only gift he left behind was his name. Another brother born three months later, the sixth boy, was named Nick, so that even while the family mourned, no one could forget.

My father tells endless stories of his childhood, of the tricks he played and horses he rode bareback and skunks he trapped. And he tells of a land so fierce that even in the midst of drought, white-faced cows, saddled horses, and little boys get caught, suck air one last time, and sink in the rush of cloudy waters.

~ ~ ~

For five years, rain falls like manna on my father's ranch. I am away at college, return each summer to wetness. I listen to my professors lecture on history and biology, the beauty of the written word. I try to apply these ideas to what I know. Grass. Endless sky. The first snuffling love of a mother cow.

When I come home to visit, the sweet smell of April is pushing up through winter snow. They are healing, these five years of wet springs, a time of plenty, of grass up to the horses' bellies, bales of hay stacked all the way to God. I listen to the pounding of the river in the night. The drought and emptiness are gone. My boots clump with slippery black gumbo, not dust, and instead of grasshoppers, I can't help but scrunch wet, gray toads beneath my heels.

Because I'm gone much of the year, inevitably I become an outsider. I return every summer, but I am not considered the same. Mrs. Lebeda nods her head and frowns, uncertain, when I say hello in the grocery store. I can see she doesn't remember me. Children I used to know look through me on Murdo's main street. I know what it is to grow invisible slowly. I know what a stranger feels, walking down a small-town street.

But being an outsider makes me look harder, at people

and places I took for granted before. I see that the prairie is beautiful, something I had always known but can now explain. The soft green hillsides, plum blossoms, and songbirds. Alfalfa hay drying in the sun, calves grown strong on sweet spring grass. The nights are louder than the days, filled with the calls of bullfrogs, crickets, locusts, owls, and coyotes. The prairie has come alive for me. Was my memory wrong—had the dust that caked and coated and hid never really existed, were my struggles to fit into this prairie, this family, just my imagination?

After five years of undergraduate classes, I graduated and came home to stay. That's what I had planned, at least. I packed everything I owned back into my truck and trailer. Old horse-show ribbons and college compositions. Clothes that I planned to wear again someday, boxes full of books with shiny covers—unread. What that trailer really held was a load of dreams, too many to hold in both cupped hands.

My horse-breeding business was a reality. The first foals were born, stretching their tiny, silver muzzles down toward the spring grass as if they could reach it. Their necks weren't as long as their legs, though, so they drank their mothers' milk instead and waited for the day the grass would come to them. And I trusted that it would.

I saw all this and saw that South Dakota was a beautiful place.

Then suddenly the rains stopped. Grasshoppers returned to eat the grass down to brown roots, the paint from fences and cars. Fields blew and the dust covered everything. Blizzards descended from the north like the wrath of God. The calm White River raged and ate away the land.

~ ~ ~

The land, our very lives, are parched and flooded by turns, perched at the bank of the river where the ground keeps crumbling away. And there we balance.

I am six again as I write this, scared of thunderstorms and the coming of the Lord. I am ten. I am fifteen, hearing about my brother Paul for the first time. I am seventeen and leaving for college, full of hope. I am twenty-nine, an adult, and living it once again, experiencing a late spring blizzard's bitter losses and the wonder of a new foal. Each birth is a miracle. There have been new droughts and floods, and I am no longer just remembering the dust and despair.

I have helped sign away our cattle and machinery. I have looked up from numbers on paper into the banker's eyes and had nothing to say. I understand more about our silences and the words that hide them. I understand about the balances all around us, between words said and unsaid, hurts imagined and real.

Each night the wind pushes up against my window, on its way from conversations with dried grasses and lonely trees. The sound is hollow, the space between two blades of grass; it speaks of distant clouds, unsettled skies.

In these times of hardship, of little rain, my father tells his stories to me again. Tells about his childhood, and sometimes, about mine. I've heard most of the stories before, but I listen again, settle deeper into my chair, into my place in this family with all its stories and silences and dry, empty spaces.

The sound of his voice is like the rain.

COYOTE

At night I dream of coyotes. Coats wheat yellow or the dark of burning sage, sleek and long of leg, throats opened to the sky. Their shadows line the bare shale bluffs of my family's South Dakota ranch, line the edges of my dreams, waiting, watching with their hungry eyes.

~ ~ ~

The summer I was seven, my father's foreman and hired hands shot coyotes, sometimes three or four a week. Howard and Cal trapped the ones they could not shoot. They ran others into the hard, black ground with their trucks, rolling the coyotes under the tires and spitting them back up into the air like clods of dirt. Then they strung the skins onto a length of baling wire stretched across the kitchen of an abandoned house.

I remember walking into that house in the dead of summer, smelling blood, red-hot and sour, beating flies from the corners of my eyes. The skins dried stiff and yellow, with four hollow tubes for legs, faces frozen stiff into a mask, and emptiness for eyes. I walked through that room with Shane, who was Howard's son, and the coyotes' tails hung down to brush our faces. We closed our eyes and groped, felt the tails against our skin, reaching soft and supple from above like the limbs of willows.

We both jumped when Cal crept silently to the window and howled through his teeth, fake and long and high. We ran out of that forest of skins, laughing and scared at the same time, and did not go back.

That same summer Shane showed me a live coyote living in a stooping box of mesh and wood in Cal's yard. I wouldn't step too close, so he poked her through the narrow wires. She didn't move, didn't look like the live coyotes I'd seen frozen in the headlights, or loping across the dog-town pasture just after dawn. She looked dead, like the skins, except for her eyes, which were fixed on something, some hill or tree or bird outside the cage. When I looked in the same direction, though, I saw nothing. Something in that stare scared me, that and the musky stench of urine dripping from the corner of the cage into a can. Cal used her urine to lure other coyotes to his steel-toothed traps.

That coyote died soon after, her coat dry as an old horse-hair brush, and no longer any use. Cal didn't even skin her. He laughed when I asked why; he was tall above me with his black hair and crooked nose and teeth, and I felt small. He said she stank too much to touch.

Later that year, when I'd see a coyote frozen in knee-high

summer grasses, or a half-grown coyote pup trotting down a draw, nosing at the ground like a yellow dog, I'd wonder about the coyote in the box. About the way Howard would throw bits of jerky from the window of his truck for Patches, my favorite of the ranch dogs, then tell me about the time he roped a coyote, strung his lariat to the bumper of the truck, and dragged her seven miles down a gravel road.

Sometimes I'd hear Patches howling along with the coyotes at night, and the line between tame and wild, between right and wrong, stretched thin.

This is when the dreams began. Some nights I ran across moonlit prairie, dried buffalo grass and sagewort crisping under the bare soles of my feet. The shale bluffs around me rippled with the silent forms of running coyotes and mule deer, jackrabbits, bobcats, and tiny swift foxes. A prairie fire crackled behind us, swallowing night and sky and dirt. One by one, the animals fell behind. There was smoke, the light and dark of burning flesh, and then I ran alone.

There were other dreams, dark, stinking dreams of death and glowing eyes. Dreams from which I woke up shaking in the middle of the night. I still have dreams where I chase but never catch a coyote's black-tipped tail; dreams that wail from inside rock and wire and wood, where there is, and always will be, a coyote living in a box.

~ ~ ~

I tried to understand cruelty as something separate from myself, from our many dogs and cats and horses. Tried to believe that somehow coyotes, badgers, and foxes didn't count, didn't feel the pain of traps or leaden shot as Patches or the soft-eyed rabbits in their cage might . . . that wild was the other side of tame, something to change or kill.

When I was twelve, Howard's oldest son, Monty, showed me how to break a mustang colt. He'd bought the colt from Russ Hawkins, our wild, bearded neighbor who ran his mares out with five hundred woolly buffalo. The colt was wild, too, a muddy brown with rolling eyes and rust around his nose and flank. He stood, trembling, on three legs. One hind foot was hitched up tight to his hairy belly with a loop of cotton rope. That rope snugged up across his withers in a knot, and another circled round his neck just behind his shaggy ears.

Even hobbled, the colt was beautiful. His neck arched up from the ropes around his withers, and his eyes were wild, full of the fast-moving clouds that race along the prairie sky.

"Easy, colt, now don't you move," Monty said, his voice low and calm, running like the slow, white water of our river, into the mustang's ears.

"It doesn't matter what I say to him as long as I keep talking," he said in that same voice, and now he'd reached the horse end of the rope.

The colt stood as Monty touched him, first on the sweaty neck, then down to rub his back and chest. His eyes moved, though, and there was terror in the white-edged way they followed Monty's every move.

When Monty reached back for the red, wool saddle

blanket he had swung up on the fence, the colt sprang suddenly, almost on top of Monty. All was dust and tangled mane and tail for a moment, then the colt was down and Monty was hatless and sitting on his head. He had a halter and a lead on the colt so fast I couldn't see his callused fingers move.

When Monty got up, the colt grunted and scrambled to his feet, tried to run on his three good legs. Monty pulled the halter rope hard and the colt fell. The colt jumped up again, and I saw the lather on his neck had turned to bloody foam. Once more he tried to run, but the ropes pulled him down and this time he lay there, eyes wide and blank, breathing wretched, panicked whinnies through his open mouth.

Monty was gentle after this. He rubbed Furacin into rope burns on the colt's neck and legs.

"See how easy, Andy-Pandy?" he asked me, and cinched the saddle slowly, eased a rawhide bosal over the colt's nose. But the mustang's eyes never changed. Months later, when we would ride out to check the calves, I'd hold that colt's reins while Monty or Cal wrote up a tag and punched it through a newborn ear. I'd rub the mustang's head, reach for an apple I'd saved for my horse Dollar, but he wouldn't even see me. His eyes were dark and hard and far away, and the part of him that had run on twelve thousand empty acres, I never saw again.

~ ~ ~

I dream about coyotes because there is so little wild left. Soon, the South Dakota prairie may be tenanted only with the hollow ghosts of sheep and cattle, the wind's lonely predawn music strumming miles of barbed-wire fence.

The bobcats are hiding, if they still exist here at all. I have seen one tiny, black-tailed swift fox in my fifteen years of watching, and the next day he was gone. There was rumor of a wolf shot trotting across an open field in western Minnesota. My father believes that wolf may have traveled through Dakota, too. Jerry Kirk, one of my father's temporary hands, swore he saw a wolf one morning on the wild south side of the river. He didn't get his rifle out quick enough, he said, and when he looked again, the wolf was gone.

The fire that is progress, that is hatred of the wild, has consumed these predators and spit them back to ash. Their lands are diminishing, closing down into a box. Sometimes even on the prairie the coyotes are silent, leaving just the stars and blue black night, the rolling of the grass to meet the dawn, the shadow of a soul pursued hidden in a thousand hills.

～ ～ ～

At night, at least, all is as it was when I was a child. I cannot see the river's newest crick and curve, the new calving shed humped up against the sky down on the bull-tail bottom. I am home from school only for the weekend, but every night, I walk the narrow path out to the gravel pit and sit down in my favorite spot, a mound overlooking the silent water. When I have been there for a while, and if I'm quiet, the coyotes begin to sing. One voice at first, a bark bleeding into wail, then a strange harmony of three voices, an octave higher than before. Though I know it's unlikely, I want to think one of those voices is Clyde's, a smoke-colored coyote I often think and dream about, for she is the only one I've known by name.

She was real, my father's pet, captured as a pup and kept because of the beauty of her silver coat. This was back when my memories were forming, still as milky and hazy as a new-born foal's eyes.

I remember Clyde because of the sadness of her yellow eyes, and because I was not allowed to touch her and wanted to so much. She lived in our front yard, chained to the trunk of a massive Chinese elm. And although she ate dog food from a plastic bowl, in her heart she was still wild. On nights when coyotes howled from the bluffs behind the house, I would sneak into the kitchen to watch Clyde writhe and dance in the moonlight, linked to earth only by the soldered length of chain.

She would lean into her collar, whining along with the music of other, wilder voices, then snarl jagged, choking cries when the singing stopped. She became smaller each night, huddling into the shallow hole she'd scratched beneath the tree, shriveling into a moonlit wraith with yellow eyes fixed on the horizon.

One night she disappeared, still wearing her collar, though the chain had been unsnapped. My dad was furious, certain that someone had sneaked over during the night and set her free. Years later, he still wonders what happened to Clyde. Whether she lived on in the wild, raising litters of smoky pups with that collar still latched around her neck, or whether she was shot or trapped soon after.

When I listen to the coyotes howl, I am reminded of Clyde, and of my dreams. Sometimes when I'm sitting by the water, and there are stars glowing above and below me, I howl back, remember words I've lost in dreams. But my throat will not open in the same way that it used to, and I am left alone, knowing there is a kind of wild I cannot be.

~ ~ ~

My father calls me one morning at my apartment in Boulder, Colorado, where I am finishing graduate school. He is excited to have seen a big dog-coyote in the front lawn at daybreak. He thinks it could be tame, looking for an easy meal, so he sets out a tub of dog food. The coyote doesn't reappear the next day or the next, but my father keeps waiting. He will watch for days, maybe have the guys throw a long-dead steer out behind the house to draw a couple more.

Now that he can't easily get around the snowy hills and draws to see the wildlife, he feeds the animals shamelessly. Round bales of alfalfa for the deer are set nose down by the living-room window. A bony, black-hide carcass is left in the cornfield just behind the house. He waits at the bedroom window with binoculars, my mother says, to see the coyotes gather to their feast.

I have dreamed of coyotes mixing with the cattle for two

nights in a row, and when my father calls, I tell him this. He says there are a pair of coyotes, gray as dawn and shy, frequenting the calving pens, slinking back into the trees. But he isn't worried yet.

These coyotes have seemed content, so far, with after-birth, milk-sweet calf manure, and the dead meat lying behind the barn. As long as claiming these gifts is their only goal, my father will not shoot them. His friendship with the coyotes is based on that deadly handshake—they stay away from living calves and he leaves his rifle locked inside a cabinet in the house. He no longer, like so many other ranchers, keeps a rifle strung up inside the back window of his truck, though he used to. Years ago my father leg-trapped bobcat, beaver, coyote, and badger. He clubbed a fearless black-footed ferret once, not knowing what it was, or how rare. He used to shoot coyotes from the open window of his truck. But people change, and he has learned to appreciate the wild as well as the tame.

Last time I was home I walked about a mile past the barn to have a look at the bone pile. The coyotes had gnawed down the little mound of stillborn and scour-killed calves—the bones stripped to flags of hide, red and black and gray, waving in the prairie wind. They had also began work on the old brockle-faced cow—smooth mouthed, dry of skin and bone, and missed at last fall's cull. I was surprised at the parts of her they'd shunned: her throat, the bony stretch of hide along her back, the ear that's tagged, and all one length of ribs. These coyotes are not bone-cracking thin or they would have stripped her clean.

My father's ranch is now a testament to the fact that cattlemen and coyotes can live in peace. For the past twenty years, he has left the shelter belts and brambled ditches unmowed, reserved wild, tangled highways between plowed fields to support buffaloberry patches, mice, shrews and gophers, insects, cottontails, and grouse—the coyotes' natural fare. He no longer allows coyotes to be trapped or hunted for sport on our land. And these coyotes do not eat cats or chickens, or even newborn calves. They live a wary, watchful balance, in their rightful role of predator, cleaner of dead bones.

Coyotes are not often welcomed on the ranches in our area. Ranchers, and sheep men in particular, bear a grudge against the coyote, sometimes well founded but often not. They poison, shoot, and trap them, hang nursing females from fence posts by one hind leg as a warning to the rest. Ask any cattleman who shoots coyotes why he does so, and he'll answer, "Because they kill calves." Ask him the last time a coyote killed one of his *healthy* calves, and he may have to think for a while. If he does have an answer, he probably doesn't know for sure if the calf fell sick first and then was gnawed by coyotes. And he's not about to find out.

The war against coyotes is more a crusade of values than anything. Tame against wild, the intrinsic value of livestock over predators. Money for hides is not the issue here. In the summer, few people skin the coyotes they kill; the hide and all is left to rot. The skins are worthless in the summer, bring only twenty dollars midwinter. And South Dakota, unlike Wyoming, no longer has a bounty on each coyote killed.

The killing of coyotes holds a respected place in South Dakota society. The teenage sons of ranchers often carry their own rifles from twelve or thirteen on. They have learned from their fathers, their grandfathers, to think of coyotes the same way they do of mice in the feed room, or Russian thistle growing in the hay field. Destroying them is not cruel but necessary and sometimes even fun. The sight of a coyote trotting down a bare shale slope or loping along the reedy bottom of a draw is an invitation to a welcome bit of sport and useful entertainment on the drive to town or in the middle of a long workday. Most of these boys are careful shots, and if the coyote makes it over the hill and out of sight one day, it may not be so lucky the next day, or week, or month. In the winter, some boys chase coyotes on snowmobiles. They shoot them, or club them senseless with the butts of rifles. Even the ones that get away aren't necessarily lucky, for calories spent running in deep snow may, in a time of hunger, be the last they'll ever spend. In the spring, boys and their fathers gas or drench and burn dens full of pups. This war of attrition goes on through generations, both of coyotes and of men.

Coyotes survive, though, with the tenacity of the deep-rooted yuccas and short, thirsty sage. Tell a South Dakota rancher that his efforts may someday exterminate the coyote from his land and he'll laugh. "Hasn't yet," he'll say, and laugh some more.

There is a tough honor about these men. They are kind to children and to orphan foals, and they live off their land with as little contact with the outside world as can be managed.

When it rains, they pull their hat brims low, almost to their eyes, and carry on. In a blizzard, the calving heifers still get checked, the river ice gets chopped so the animals can drink. But in this world predators have little place or value, and eventually, must be destroyed.

Here at least, in the rolling hills and buttes of the White River valley, on my father's ranch and on some other scattered sections of this land, the fire licking at the coyote's heels, at every wild thing's heels, does not burn.

Ever since Cal left in '85, and Howard two years later, the coyotes have been coming back. They seem to know about—maybe Clyde has told them—this four-thousand-acre haven. They line up on the prairie hills, atop the ridges and the crumbling, blue shale draws, and they sing.

~ ~ ~

There is a place between dreaming and awake where something hides. I can squeeze my eyes shut some mornings, just after the alarm rings, and see the past, or maybe see a dream.

The image is grainy, blurred with time, of a little girl, her long chestnut hair swinging down her back, a darker shade than mine is today. I watch her totter down the gravel driveway, hands burrowed in her flannel gown, eyes fixed on the coyote chained in the front yard.

I still feel the sharp-edged rocks cutting through her bare soles, shiver with her in the naked night air, and when she reaches Clyde's huddled, silver body, I help her fingers find and unclip the heavy chain. Through her eyes I watch the smoke-colored coyote slink away, slowly at first, then faster, in a crazy, hump-backed gallop. I see Clyde stop, look back once with eyes like crescent moons, then slip away to shadow.

SOMETHING BURIED

I grew up looking down. Watching for fossils and snakes, cactus and agates at the same time. I rarely found the pretty stones—the swirling red-and-black patterns of Fairburns or the round gray stones that looked like any others until you broke them open, found a gold or purple crystal star inside. I usually brought home thistles and sandburs and prairie three-awn needles in my pant legs instead.

My father was the discoverer in the family. He watched the ground, too, as he walked—head down, thick, awkward hands swinging by his belt. Only the back of his head really saw the sky. But for him the ground opened, offered brilliant agates from a plowed field, blunted arrowheads and flints from the hilltop shale. From my father I learned that the sky was really buried in the soil, the rocks its stars.

Even the river conspired to help him with its slow and winding hunger. Sometimes buffalo skulls, once an ivory mammoth tooth, blue veined and thick as two fists clenched, in its powdered silt bank. Precious things, half-buried at his feet. Pioneer stoves, rusty sections of hand-twisted barbed-wire fence, a red-stone peace pipe. He found these all without really trying, just by walking, looking down.

In time, the earth began to offer me some gifts as well. My father's treasures were solid: teeth and fragments of bone, tiny arrowheads carved from quartz, sea snails curled, as if in sleep, in the center of a stone. I found more fragile reminders—glass bottles, left unbroken from the homestead days. I brought them home, one after the other, until my talent for finding glass became funny or meant something, or both.

Even now I ride upon them in unlikely corners of the prairie, in places I expect to see only cattle bunched up around a dam, the hot blue line where grass meets sky. There, at my horse's feet, will be a purpling wine bottle, unbroken, half-sunk in the washed-out soil of a draw. Or I'll be walking in the willows down by the river and find a squat glass bottle made to hold ink—square and thick-waisted—buried in a drift of river sand. In the fields behind the house I'll unearth long-necked brown bottles whose corks have rotted into loam.

I imagine these bottles full of sweet and noxious things— green liniment or hair tonic or the greasy gold of cod-liver oil. To a deeply religious Dutch Reformed soul these bottles may have meant something else. Maybe this one held rye whiskey that looked like dirty water until it touched your lips; musty yellow corncob beer; the purple sin of choke-cherry wine.

These bottles are a record of human life on the plains.

They were tossed out whole into the prairie sea. Now they are empty except for memories, which is a kind of message, I suppose. They lie buried in the soil, uneasy as questions.

I still look down when I'm riding the trout dam pasture or walking along the riverbank. I'm searching for something long buried, for answers to a question I can't put into words. Glass bottles, hollow and shifting colors in the sun, are what I find.

~ ~ ~

Prairie grass covers, it rolls unending, green and gold. Underneath there are rocks and glass and bones and lives lived in the dark. There are earthworms, moles, gophers, and dung beetles. Rattlesnakes, shrews, and soft, milky-white grubs. Cutworms nestled alongside the roots of corn and yuccas and cottonwood trees.

There will always be something left behind, shards of a life we try to piece together again. Maybe it's the dented metal portrait of Sleepy Eye, chief of the Wahpeton Lakota Sioux in 1834. My father found the painting hidden inside the curling tin walls of a homestead shack. The portrait— sun-weathered face, full of wisdom, with droopy eyelids and a rosebud hanging from the eagle feather in his hair— is surrounded by scenes from the old chief's life: a buffalo hunt, a pony falling, a peace pipe. From these scenes I spent hours as a child recreating his life.

Maybe what's left behind are bones. The skeleton of a buffalo, long dead, emerging from a shale cliff. A skull with sharply curving horns half submerged in river water. There are stories passed down from generation to generation. Secrets are buried, too, like the bones of a child carried away in a flood, unseen but remembered. They will never melt away.

~ ~ ~

The one thing buried my father has never found is a jar full of pennies he hid as a child—his own small treasure, sealed up tight in a mason jar.

He buried it in the yard of the abandoned Martin place, up on the flats near Okaton, where he grew up. He said he dug deep, hitting tree roots and gravelly soil before he quit. He'd marked the spot with a scrawny sapling growing nearby.

We go out to find the jar when I am fourteen. I pretend not to listen to the story of how he buried his treasure and expected to dig it up again in a week, or maybe a month. It's been forty-five years. I am listening.

We walk together across my Uncle Ned's fallowed wheat. My father in his long-sleeved summer shirt and old brown pants, carrying a shovel, me in shorts and worn-through tennis shoes. I've got the old posthole digger, the one with both wooden handles snapped off not far above the blades.

The yard is hard to find. No one has lived in the Martin homestead for over fifty years. Grass grows waist high, dried husks of sweet clover and last year's ragweeds clog the yard.

I explore, though there's not much to see beyond the rotting shingles, old chicken wire, and broken plaster walls. An elm tree straggles shade over it all.

"This might be the place," my father says, and plants his shovel in a stretch of kochia weed. He is not far from the elm tree. I take a shallow bite of soil with the digger, not far from him. A little closer to the tree. Soon a rhythm is starting. Punch into the ground, pull the splintered handles, draw the little mouthful of dirt up alongside the hole. Again. Suddenly there is the chime of metal on glass. I drop the posthole digger and hunch down to look.

"I've found something!" I reach down to scrabble with my naked hands. I pull up a ridged blue oval, tamped tight with soil. An old telephone insulator. Made, of course, of glass.

"Oh darn. It's nothing." I click my tongue and roll my eyes, but I put it in my pocket.

Next my father finds a handmade nail, a hinge, rusted thin, and two curving iron doors, stamped with "H. B. Wells." He says they're from a wood-burning stove. He throws one of the doors in the back of the truck.

I dig up a leather boot sole, nearly mummified from damp. Some thread-thin earthworms, broken pieces from a china plate, and finally, a thick brown bottle with a center seam. Along its curving base are two dozen cold, sleeping grubs. I leave them curled in soft, white balls.

"Look at this," my father says. He is holding a handful of dirt, black and soft against his callused palm.

"What?" I say, looking closer. It must be something really small. I still don't see.

"It's good ground here, fertile." I roll my eyes again, but keep looking. "See how dark, these crumbly bits of old, dead leaves? Full of worms, too."

I grunt and shuffle back to my posthole digger to look for coins. But I don't forget. Only a farmer would search for treasure and find it in the cold black soil itself.

We never find the jar of coins. But I don't really care so much by the time we leave. My pockets are bulging with forgotten treasures, and there is dirt jammed up black beneath my fingernails. I cradle the old brown bottle on my lap the whole way home. It is enough.

~ ~ ~

Deep in a shale hillside, along the gravel road that leads past the chokecherry thickets, there is the white gleam of bone. You can see it from the road, and you slip through the barbed-wire fence to stand directly underneath, but the skeleton is surprisingly inaccessible—ten feet down from where the sod has cut away, thirty feet up from the grassy bottom of the draw. A blip of white in a vertical sweep of crumbling, gray soil.

My sister spotted the skeleton on a hot day in September, when I was home from college for the weekend. We try to climb the hill to see what kind of animal could have left those bones, but the hillside keeps shivering away, and we slide twice as far as we've just climbed, leaving dark wedges where our feet have been.

Finally I make it close enough to reach one porous elbow of bone.

"Careful, Ann," Brenda warns from her perch just below me. "Don't break them."

I balance by planting my feet against Brenda's back. She groans but is laughing at the same time.

Brenda is hunched over, pointing down the hill, so she can't see what I'm sweeping from the dirt. There is a massive leg bone, a femur I think, and a whole vertebral column, disarticulated, and coiled like a snake. I dig out a vertebra and blow on it. The bone is light and porous, as big around as my palm. It feels cold and gray, there in my hand, somewhere it does not belong.

"I think this is an axial bone," I say, handing it carefully down.

"Not fossilized," Brenda says. "Buffalo, I think. Pretty old, though." After turning the vertebra this way and that, she hands the bone back to me. I wedge it back in place and lean back to look. The skeleton looks disarrayed somehow, the earth around it weeping blood-dark soil.

Brenda turns to look up, too, and suddenly we are sliding backwards down the shale bank. We are both scrabbling at the quick gray shale, shaking with laughter. I look up as I'm sliding. The bones stay just the same as we become smaller, it seems. The bottom finally comes.

We slap dust from each other, then stand in knee-deep grass, looking up. The skeleton shimmers out of shadow.

"Guess we'll just leave it there," Brenda says, looking over at me. There is a gray streak of dust from her forehead to nose.

"Guess we will." And I am relieved.

It was probably a buffalo. I know that now. But standing at the bottom of the hill that day, covered with dust, I realized I liked not knowing.

Those of us born to families who work the land sometimes forget that some soil should be left unturned. Full of dark, mysterious life and untouched places.

The next rain would wash away our footprints, maybe tumble the vertabrae, one by one, into the bottom of the draw. Then another rain, and another and another, might cover them again, so that the animal that lived and died on that hill would remain a mystery, forever out of sight. There is always something buried.

~ ~ ~

All good farmers know that there is a limit to how deep you can dig and still find fertile soil. This is called the lime, or white, line from the residue of limestone that accumulates there. This line marks the boundary between fertile and hardpan soil. Rain will not soak past this point—the more topsoil, the deeper the white line.

In some places you could dig to the white line with the sharp metal teeth of the plow. The ground is so hard the tractor shakes, burns oil in hot, black gasps, and the field's almost not worth planting, but you've long since torn away its grasses, and so the digging goes on.

Even drought-resistant sorghum, so dark green it looks almost black, won't grow tall and slick in these fields. Plants send roots down only so far, to that line limit. Rocks divide themselves between fertile soil and not, above and below. But all things living exist above. All wheat, corn, even sorghum, grown only to be fermented in the silage pit, respect this line. Limitations.

In horses' feet there are boundaries, too. Also called the white line, this place is the chalky border dividing living, blood-fed hoof from the hard outer shell a horse can walk on.

A young farrier, just out of school, once trimmed my four heavily pregnant broodmares too short, nipping up into their white line. The hooves looked fine, rasped to shiny, flint-colored ovals. But in the morning, when I poured oats out in the trough, the mares didn't move from their huddle in the middle of the paddock. Heads down, long manes whipping into their eyes, each one's four feet sorely planted. They watched me pour grain—yesterday there had been such hunger and excitement, old matriarch Pine flashing her heels at the rest—and now none moved. When I reached for Pine's front foot she shuddered, a horse shot, blown through with pain. Her hoof was hot, and when I'd picked out the clammy dirt and fresh manure, her white line was visible, pink with seeping blood. The farrier came back, sheepishly, that evening to nail shoes on each of the mares so they could bear to walk to feed and water.

I know that nipping past the white line can make a sound horse stagger, three-legged lame, after stepping on a rounded pebble. That mistake can dredge fresh blood from pasture-dried hooves, hooves tough and black as wind-blown wood.

I come up against my own white lines, where the truth is buried deeper than I can reach. Digging for it hurts, like walking barefoot in the spring when your soles are tender as a scar's pink new skin, so that even the rockless prairie soil pricks up through your heels. Every pebble feels like a boulder, edges raw on tender skin.

I walk a careful line to know what to uncover. What to leave buried.

~ ~ ~

After a long night walk along the edges of a field, I sit down on the front lawn to pull off my shoes.

I like to walk at night, to think and sort things out. Life becomes clear to me sometimes at night, when more is hidden.

I am beginning to understand why my parents never talked about my brother Paul. Why his bones stayed buried, more than six feet down. It is because he lives on, in a sense, in this soil and its yellowed grasses. In the sky and the steer grazing beyond the barbed-wire fence; in the tiny ridge of anklebone beneath my boot and in my freckled skin. My mother's grief became flesh; I was knitted from her tears.

I start to untie my shoes. My fingers meet pricks and edges—my socks are a cluster of prickly sandburs. I pull the burrs away, drop them in a careful pile. These are my reminders to walk looking down. But there is something more. I lie back on the grass. The stars, impossibly bright in the wide night sky, are my reminders to look up.

~ ~ ~

I'm not the discoverer in the family, at least not of solid, ancient things. Perhaps it is because I don't really want to know all that is hidden. The hollow gleam of glass is as close as the prairie will ever come to offering me its secrets, in bottles that I am left to fill with more questions, never answers.

The precious stones will stay, half-buried, at my feet. There are mysteries, arrowheads buried in dark and secret places, baby boys who will be spoken of in whispers. I walk on. There is always something buried.

SNAKES AND SALVATION

One of the things modern medicine has managed to do besides turning hospitals into churches and doctors into priests, is to infect the culture with the foreknowledge of distantly imminent death, something human beings don't really have it in them to cope with. What I mean is, we are supposed to live knowing we are going to die; we are not supposed to live knowing when.

—James Galvin, *The Meadow*

You have to be ready to die alone when you live seventy miles from the nearest hospital. There's no telling when. There's snakebite and lightning strikes, sickle blades and solitary heart attacks. All it takes is one good kick from a two-year-old filly you thought you knew and you're on your back, caught in God's bright staring eye. Your horse slips going down a hill, the cow whose calf you're tagging charges head down, faster than you can jump away—there won't be an ambulance or priest. Praying might be all that's left, God's grace the only cure.

Where I grew up, hospitals were far away, but God was always near.

It can happen this fast. When I was six years old, Clayton Baxter reached into the oats barrel for the coffee-can scoop and was bitten. Two times, fast as lightning. He sat down then and there to die. He was an old man, snakebit, far from home. He and Howard had ridden horses instead of driving a pickup, and it was five miles of sunburned hills and draws back to the ranch.

Clayton was small and hard and wrinkled, like a walnut's shell. He walked with bowed knees, wearing down just the outsides of his boot soles, and his step was silent on the hardest ground. He worked for my father for five years, starting when he was seventy-five, and I was just learning to ride a bike without its training wheels. Back then I might even have pictured God like him, wrinkled and wise, with thick white hair and an honest, sun-dried squint.

Clayton knew things God might, too. How to talk a wild filly gentle or read the coming winter in a beaver's thickened dam; which red-throated prairie flowers could kill a hungry cow, and which would help her grow a calf come spring. He prayed and roped with equal pleasure, carried a fencing pliers and a cardboard-cover Bible in the pocket of his coat.

Clayton told me later that he talked to God that day, in the shadow of the shack. He'd repented long ago, was saved and born again, so he was ready when death came hissing from a can of oats.

It had been a long, hot day in July, perfect for checking the black herd, which grazed the AI pasture, named for the corrals where we bred cattle using artificial insemination. Howard and Clayton stopped at the shack standing near the old corrals to water their horses and cool down in the shade. It was just two men and two horses—Clayton's mare, Ginger, fast, but twelve years old already; Howard's Gem, a short-legged nag, too slow for the run back home.

Howard was outside, smoothing Furacin into a saddle sore rubbed behind Gem's elbow. He heard Clayton's scream, an old man's breath, let out all at once. Howard said later it was really just a sigh, surprised, then resigned. But I like to think it was a scream, such as I would have given, feeling fangs sunk in between thumb and finger, the sinuous curl of snake hidden in the cool, shifting oats.

There was no time to think. Howard chose Ginger, cinched her back up tight in one jerk, and galloped off in a haze of dust. This mad gallop must have been hard for Howard, who never ran a horse hard, to its bottom, who always told my sister and me to walk our horses the last mile home, never put them up still sweating anywhere but beneath the saddle. But that day he ran Ginger the whole five miles to the ranch, leaving behind gates strung open and scattered, like a child's toys. He might have killed her with that wild run, but he had no choice. He was younger, maybe not so sure of himself back then. Fear must have showed on his clean-shaved face, in the way he used the leather reins as a quirt, to beat a running horse. Was he wondering all the time if it were too late already? Would Ginger make it? Was she fast enough?

They must have nearly flown over the hills and draws and deep, brown cattle trails, jumped yuccas and slid down black shale banks with Ginger's hocks jammed nearly to her knees. That's the only way he could have made it in the time he did. Afterward he left the mare heaving, lathered white, outside the barn. Still saddled, nearly foundered, but alive. She would have run on, he said later, almost like she knew.

He made it back up in the diesel in hardly any time at all, to rescue an old man he hoped was still breathing, propped up against the shack with his hand swelled into a ball, a fist twice the size of his heart.

Clayton knew he was going to die. This is what haunts me about the story—an old man stretched out in the only shade around, next to a splintering old shack and wooden corrals nobody would ever repair, alone with his knowing, at the mercy of God.

But he didn't die. His hand and arm never swelled to black, his heart didn't start to jump and pound and race with poison.

Turns out he was bitten by a bull snake, venom harmless as a honeybee's. But still, imagine what you would think up there on the lonely topland, just you and someone else's slow horse to watch you die, five hundred staring cows gathered down around the dam, looking up the mud slope at you. And all you can see is the hot blue sky, the stamped mud up to the salt lick, red paint licking down the splintered walls of the shack. Clayton must have looked down at those snakebite holes in his hand and prayed.

Clayton said later he had plenty of time to remember all

he'd done wrong and just enough time to make sure he was sorry when Howard came flying over the saddleback draw cross-country, tires spinning more on air than grass.

~ ~ ~

A paramedic I know, a friend of a friend, put it this way: there are two types of people in the world—urban and rural.

Urbanites are dependent, quick to call 911 for help. They are used to being around people; people are their number-one resource. Hospitals are where you go when you need help. Doctors stand between you or your husband or wife or son and death; doctors are a stand-in for God.

Rural people, on the other hand, hate to ask for help. They are self-sufficient, both because they want to be and because they have no choice. When disaster strikes, they're more likely to call on God, or just themselves, than on 911.

The difference is a canyon, a split that's deep and wide. It might be called the difference between east and west, but it's not that simple.

~ ~ ~

There's nothing like a rattlesnake to make you think of life and death.

The buzz of a rattler is unmistakable, like fear wound tight. It is a sound that can bring you face to face with God. Someone visiting the prairie for the first time will hear a rattler in every clump of grass, every locust's whir. But no one who has heard a rattler once will forget its buzz, or mistake that impossible buzz for a locust, for anything else in the world but a snake.

To tell the truth, you have to be old or young or pretty unlucky to die from a rattlesnake bite. Depends on where you're bitten, and how long it takes to get to town.

My first dealings with snakes were shaped from the basic teachings of a rancher's cow-centered universe: Rattlesnakes hurt cattle; therefore, they are evil. They must be destroyed before they somehow destroy us. There is a hard-line religion to this statement. Resist the devil and he will flee from you. No. Better. Resist the devil, and, if you're strong enough, bash his head in, too. For who needs a devil at all, a balance, if there is a God. Evil must be overcome.

Rattlers, at least, unlike most forms of evil I've known, give warning. They're peaceable enough as snakes go, mostly trying to avoid being stepped on. In fact, most harmless snakes, when cornered, will put on as fierce a show as a rattler, without the noise—or the venom. And while a rattler's buzz means "Watch out!" to the wary, others, who don't understand, come closer to sniff and explore. And that buzzing reaches up to snag them.

Young cattle and horses are especially at risk. They hear the buzzing, like a locust gone wild. It is a seductive, intoxicating sound. Cattle are easy targets, with their simple-minded curiosity, their meaty jowls and thick, damp muzzles. Nearly always the victim is a calf or yearling heifer, playful, curious, with wide-lashed eyes, ears quivering forward as she reaches to sniff the snake, that humming near the yucca spikes. She snorts, again, head down, at that fizzing in the grass. It moves! She spooks backward, then approaches again. The snake strikes.

You come upon her a few days later, a snake-bit heifer, her head swollen sideways with poison. You can hear her breathing from over the next hill, louder than the clopping of your horse's feet, the saddle leather's creak. She stands head down, maybe bogged down in the cloven mud along the dam. She's black, her spine hunched up and a gray mass of flies writhing on it. Her eyes are small, look far away. Her head is lopsided, as wide as it is long. The snake bit her just below the jowl. Her breath rasps in and out of a burning hole the size of a straw.

She may very well live without any help. Mostly they do. But there's that look in her eye. She's giving up. You have to save her. Penicillin, anti-inflammatories. Glucose. A hollow needle pushed into her jaw, to let the poison out.

Most of the snakes I've seen lie in full stretch on the gravel road, or curl up in a yucca's shade, near the bare lip of a draw or cattle trail on a shale hillside. We kill them as they run away, throw rocks at their narrow bodies until they are forced to curl and face, ready to attack their attackers.

The whole world around me killed snakes when I was a child. Howard, Cal, Shane, Monty, Brenda, my father. Everyone I knew. Even my mother, once, when she stepped out of the car after pulling it into the garage, and heard something buzzing so loudly she thought it was a helicopter passing overhead. It was a huge rattlesnake, coiled thick and brown on the step just beneath the kitchen door. While Brenda, David, and I watched from the backseat my mother grabbed a garden rake and beat the snake to death. Afterward, she carried it looped over the rake out into the yard and covered it with a trash barrel. Only then would she let us out of the car. She was shaking, and there was blood on her soft, white shoes.

I killed rattlesnakes, too. Some for no other reason than they were there, in the grass at my horse's feet, rattling a warning I didn't want to hear. I never could learn to aim very well with a rope, so I killed snakes with whatever I could find. I would yank the back cinch off my saddle, beat the snake's wedge-shaped head with the cinch's heavy buckle, until there was nothing left to crush.

I once took the bridle off my bay mare Pine and beat a snake to blood with the bit. This happened up in a corner of the beaver slide pasture, on top of a hill where cattle seldom grazed because there was little grass. It was a bare place by some yuccas where I knew snakes lived. I don't know why I'd come that way in the first place, if not to find a snake.

I swung the bridle by its leather reins, holding Pine by her tie-down strap. She stood back hard at the end of that strap, nostrils wide, spooking with each thud. She nearly jerked away with my final blow, and was still rattling breath out through her nostrils when I stepped back from the snake. I stood for a minute, telling the story to myself a few times in practice.

"It was a big one, right under Pine's feet. All I had was the bridle, so I used that . . ."

Suddenly, in one of those perfectly clear moments that comes when you least expect it, I realized that my audience was a scared horse and my victim a broken slip of snake, beaten so bloody you couldn't be sure what it had once been. I saw myself as if from a distance: faded jeans and a worn-out, snap-down shirt handed down from my brother; strong freckled hands, hair swept up under a MoorMan's Feed cap. I could have been one of the guys. From a distance, I might have looked exactly like Shane or Monty when they were killing a snake, and afterward, I might have sounded like them, too.

I didn't take the rattles, though they were long enough. I put the bit back in Pine's mouth and steered her down the hill. She reined hard, like a colt not broke to the bit. Later, when Howard asked about my day, I mumbled something about finding a cow/calf pair outside the fence, and how hot it had been, even in the shade. I didn't tell him about the snake.

As an adult, I have come to a kind of truce with the prairie's rattlesnakes, and, with it, an understanding of the risk of living and the threat of dying.

I still shiver at the sight of rattlesnakes. My toes and fingers itch when I hear a buzzing in the grass, and my stomach knots into a quiver of its own. But I kill only those that are a direct threat to my life or my family's, or those that threaten areas heavily grazed by the cattle or horses, such as the bottoms around the barn. My father sees this truce as foolish, on a level with another woman's fateful dealings with another, larger snake. But I haven't had to kill a snake in eight years.

I am not afraid to die here, on my father's land. I hope it doesn't happen soon, but I think I'll be as ready as I can be when it does. I'm careful but not afraid. I check barrels before plunging my hand inside, keep my eyes on the packed dirt around gates and on the high, open places, which snakes like so well. I don't go looking for snakes anymore just to kill them. It's enough to know they are there.

PREDATORS AND PREY

Already there are meadowlarks, up before the sun. I hear their thick voices from my drowse inside the warm truck. I open my eyes. Outside the window, deer are still browsing stray clumps of alfalfa along the road. I can barely make them out. It's almost 5 A.M. By the time we climb out of the valley and bump over ten miles of dirt road to the AI pasture's gate, half the sky will be orange.

Brenda is beside me, next to Howard who is driving and teaching her to shift. He punches the clutch in with his cracking yellow boot; she shoves the straight metal-knobbed stick up and over.

"That's third. It works in an H shape, for Howard," he says and smiles over at me, because it will be my turn on the way back. Brenda is already almost an expert, having driven the truck and trailer once on a flat stretch of dirt road outside the trout dam pasture.

"Why do I always have to get the gate?" I grumble on my way out the door. Brenda always finds a way to sit in the middle. This is an easy gate, the wire not stretched tight, mainly so I can open it. I close the gate and jump back in. Brenda sticks her tongue out at me.

"First," Howard says, and Brenda turns back to her job.

*My job is scouting out the ranch horses. They graze in a band,
usually just over the hill from the shack and corrals. I see them first,
as usual. Susie and Pride, the two I ride, are grazing by themselves,
down toward the dam. Bonnie, Peaches, Lightning, and Rosie, the
bossy group of dun and buckskin mares that Brenda, Howard, or
Howard's son Shane usually ride, are off alone. The rest are ranch
geldings—blaze-faced sorrels and bays that don't care who they
graze with. The herd is trained to head for the corrals when they
hear the truck's horn, but sometimes, like today, we have to drive
out to them, the truck jerking over cactus and rutted cattle trails.
I get to kick Brenda in the knee as I'm leaning out the window.*

*"Get on there, horses!" I yell. "Come on Susie, Pride, lead them
in!" They look up blinking, then the mares squeal and whirl around
on their haunches, and the whole herd jackknifes off the hill, tails
kinked over their backs. Susie and Pride don't break a trot, and
Howard honks at their short, brown tails the whole way in.*

*When we get back down to the shack, I run for a bucket of oats
and pour it down the trough in the horse pen. I get out quick, too,
since horses are stirred up after a run, and Bonnie and Lightning
are sure to be kicking at the geldings.*

*After that we sit for a while and watch the cattle at the catfish
dam, just down from the shack. Howard opens the coffee thermos,
and I drink some because Brenda does, pretending to like it hot out
of the plastic lid. Luckily there are gingersnaps to go along.*

*Brenda whispers to me as I'm taking a sip, "Don't you know
this is the same thermos we heat the bull semen in?" I look into
my cup. The coffee inside is dark and mysterious, a shimmer of
oil floating on top. I eat some more gingersnaps and blow damp
crumbs at her.*

We sit there another twenty minutes while the horses finish their oats. There are meadowlarks behind us in the grass, and the first killdeer of the day screeches, glides by on her worried, stilted legs.

Howard is telling three-wheeler jokes, the kind where the old cowboy is stuck, perched on a Honda that's half sunk in a muddy draw, water coming up around all three tires. His horse is on top of the hill, looking down and laughing. Howard's using his best Mississippi accent to tell the jokes, and Brenda and I laugh together. I'm learning to draw cartoon three-wheelers. I already have horses down and can draw a fair cowboy, though he always ends up looking just like Howard. If the cartoon turns out good enough, Howard says he'll send it in to Western Horseman magazine.

Howard knows more than anyone about breaking colts, working cattle, fixing diesel engines, braiding bridles and reins. You name it. I'm learning almost as much as Brenda from him now. He used to think I was too little to ride out alone with him and Lightning, his blaze-faced mare, to bring in a rank pair or cut a water-belly bull out of the dog-town pasture herd. But now, sometimes, when Brenda's gone he takes me along. Last week I learned how to dig up black sampson root and chew it for a toothache. He showed me how to work a five-cord braid into a pair of roping reins. I don't have that down quite yet, but I'm not telling Brenda that I'm learning. She can't braid tack.

It's getting hot, the dew burned clear off the grass and fences by now, so we get up to catch the horses. Brenda and Howard walk off, still talking about three-wheelers and ways that horses are better. I'm daydreaming, standing by the shack with Susie's old leather bridle in my hands, thinking about what color parachute cord I'll pick for braiding her new bridle. This is the moment when I first see *a weasel, and he's gone so fast I can't be sure of what I've seen. Something red and supple, winding through the gap between the wooden chute and headgate. I start to yell for Brenda, then stop myself. She won't believe me. I check both ways down the manure-smeared chute, walk around to look under the pile of fence posts and railroad ties behind. But I see nothing, and so take Susie's bridle out to the horse pen, pass Brenda leading Bonnie, Howard dragging Peaches out the gate with a loop of twine around her yellow neck.*

The summer I turned nine, I was working up at the corrals almost regularly, like one of the guys. But I wasn't a full ranch hand yet. I got lost sometimes and had to ride for miles to find a fence line I could follow back toward the shack. I considered myself one of the cowboys, but really I was someone to drag sweaty saddle blankets down from the fence and bring them inside. I could watch for cows cycling into heat down by the dam, but needed help driving the pairs to the corral.

The Artificial Insemination season gave shape to my summer. For two months, each day could be broken into shifts. Five in the morning to noon, noon to 4 P.M., 4 P.M. to dark. We split the shifts between us—either Howard or Cal was always there in the mornings and evenings when there were cows to be bred. Shane and Monty, Howard's teenage sons, helped on days they weren't haying. I always hoped they'd stay down in the valley stacking square bales or fixing fence. That way I'd get some of the more important jobs, like trailing pairs, or helping Howard pull a cow that had gotten stuck in the dam. I preferred the evening shift, which was usually the busiest—some nights we'd still be riding when the air chilled and smelled like dam water, and the first stars were coming out. We took turns with the noon shift, which was shorter but deadly hot. Each shift the prairie was different. Black velvet sky hardening to blue by morning, staring sun all afternoon, then the pink and gathering cool of evening.

There were five hundred and fifty cows. Howard knew all their numbers from the cow/calf book he kept folded in his shirt pocket. He'd write down the ear-tag numbers of cows coming into heat, then he and Brenda would choose which ones to breed to which bulls. I watched Howard breed the cows by shoving one gloved arm up their rectum, feeling for the cervix, then cupping his other hand and sliding it into the cow along with a straw of frozen semen. The cows stood for it because there was nowhere else for them to go. They leaned up against the head catch of the chute, backs humped, heads trapped low, waiting. The calves next year would come out strange and thick, looking like Chianina bulls that lived a thousand miles away. I can still see Howard pulling off the armpit-length plastic glove—carefully, inside out—after it was covered with warm, brown manure from inside the cow. Shane would sneak the dirty gloves out of the trash barrel and drape them, still warm, over my horse's rump or withers, sometimes onto the seat of my saddle.

The world I lived in was peopled mostly by animals. There were strict rules about how they were to be treated, which ones were protected, which were tolerated, which were exterminated. There was no question of where certain animals stood in the hierarchy. For predators, the men kept rifles handy in the back windows of their pickups. Rattlesnakes were coiled and waiting at the lips of dusty draws. Coyotes slunk down hillsides like scrounging yellow dogs. The summer I turned nine there was a family of weasels living in the woodpile behind the shack. They were not afraid of us and should have been. They were quick and red, with hunger glowing in their eyes.

I learned most of what I know about ranching up at the AI corrals. It was Howard, not my father, who taught me to kill a rattlesnake with my lariat, or whatever was handy, who taught me to keep one eye shut and exhale as I squeezed the trigger of a twenty-two, trying not to think about the prairie dog belly centered in my scope.

I learned less violent skills as well—how to duck my head when my horse was galloping after a cow so I wouldn't lose my hat. I knew how fast a good horse could take a shale-banked wash—and the difference between a good horse and the ones I usually rode. I learned not to hold on to the saddle horn, which is what greenhorns do, no matter how fast my horse spun or stumbled or bolted. Sometimes I fell, but I never held the horn. I learned about losing a wild cow and calf when they were halfway through the gate, breaking my reins and having to splice them back together, going thirsty, then bloating myself sick with scratchy, iron-flecked water from the milk jug in the shack. I learned to listen to what Howard told me to do, knowing his eyes were always on me, watching, measuring. I wanted more than anything to measure up.

Brenda and I grew up working alongside the men—my father was one of those rare, even-sighted ranchers who never questioned that girls were strong and smart and tough as boys. We were lady ranchers from the start, interested in club calf shows and breaking colts above all else. My sister and I preferred horses to tractors, and certainly to makeup, dresses, and playing dolls. We looked up to the cowboys as fathers, gods. If they let us down, the earth might shatter and fall apart, and so we chose not to see when they did. When we were betrayed, we told no one, and especially not each other.

~ ~ ~

I keep coming back to the weasels. There had always been cottontails around the shack, but the guys shot those to make sure their tame rabbits wouldn't catch any diseases. These tame brown-and-white spotted rabbits came from cages behind Cal's house. They lived off weeds and oats the horses dropped.

That was until the weasels started coming around. I had first seen one, narrow, red-brown, out by the squeeze chute. Just a glimpse and it was gone. I wondered a few days what I'd seen, told Cal, who blustered about ferrets and polecats but made it sound like I hadn't seen a thing except part of a rusty fence post sticking out of the ground.

But later that week the weasel was back, sitting up on a fallen fence post outside the shack as if he belonged there.

It's morning, already hot. I can't believe what I'm seeing. The weasel is silhouetted against the sun, and even so early in the day, he ripples and shimmers like a mirage. Behind me, in the shack, a mouse scrabbles against the floor, its claws chicking and scratching in the silence. The weasel's dark amber head swivels and dips, his nose twitching, his front legs flat against his mottled yellow belly. The mouse inside the shack goes quiet. She's probably crouched inside the warm, dark refrigerator we use as shelves for extra ear tags and the orange and blue chalk paint for marking cows. The weasel leans toward me, then places one paw gently back on the post.

Shane and Cal are saddling their horses on the other side of the shack. I hear the chink of a bit against teeth, explosions of laughter.

I don't want to scare the weasel away. He is the first I've ever really seen. I stand very still, and he doesn't move, just looks back at me. Shane is inside the shack now, bragging what a good shot he is with his twenty-two. He carries it in the back window of the yellow Dodge, along with a stubbly old lariat and an oily Pioneer seed-corn cap.

Sometimes on the way home from a day checking cows he'll jam on the Dodge's brakes, slide to a stop in a cloud of dust, and lean out the window, crouching over the scope of the twenty-two. The coyotes seem to know he can't shoot straight, though. They stand, silver against the yellow-green sweet clover, while the rifle barks and bullets hit on either side with puffs of dust. Then they turn and trot away, nonchalant, as Shane swears and slaps the pickup door with his callused palm.

Somehow, while I'm listening, the weasel has inched closer to the shack, almost up to the toe of my boots. He looks intent, hungry, maybe drawn by the smell of mouse nests, or the spotted rabbits crouching under the floorboards.

Just then Cal walks around the corner, stride rolling and loose-jointed, boot heels scuffing the hard-packed ground.

"Look!" I say, turning back to point out the weasel.

Cal looks at the empty fence post and shakes his head. "Seeing more polecats, Pandy?" And steps back into the shack, laughing.

The weasel has disappeared, the only sign of his leaving a whisper of dust curling toward the sky.

I see myself as I was then, the summer of 1979. Pale, with straight hair. Sunburned arms that prickled in the bare sun. Baggy jeans, a stretchy yellow T-shirt with "Expensive" written in glittery letters across the chest. It hadn't started getting tight yet. My eyes were small and gray behind dust-speckled glasses. I thought about horses most of the time, drew pictures of wild stallions, foals scratching an ear with one hind foot, on the borders of my notebooks.

I was a ranch kid, but the truth is less romantic than it sounds. There was dust and too many grasshoppers and towering kochia weeds behind the barn. My ranch horses were always hand-me-downs—half-lame geldings who had worked a lifetime for someone else, who would never buck or bolt or dance sideways when the other riders galloped past us after crank-tailed calves.

Half the time I was sleepy or bored up at the AI pasture. I'd pick a dam, sit and watch those cows for hours, occasionally riding down for a closer look at an ear tag. Sometimes I sat at the shack, snapping a strip of old inner tube at flies snoozing on the sun-baked walls. Sometimes I just watched the rabbits, how they sat back on their haunches to lick their toes, pulled a soft white ear down for cleaning with one front paw.

When Brenda and I were both working, there was no time for sitting. It was inevitable that we would compete, each wanting to come out tougher, on top. There was no contest. Brenda knew about vaccination dates and protein requirements, even back then. At thirteen she was picking our herd sires from the American Breeders Service catalog. She rode Bonnie, a beautiful dun four-year-old mare that bit me once, that flew round in circles when Brenda un-wrapped her slicker from behind her saddle or dangled the loop of her rope down past her ankle.

My sister tanned brown, her hair glowed an impossible sunny blond, her eyes shone the clearest blue. She was quick and sure with her special purple rope. I was freckled, mouse colored, with sunburned arms and gray-specked eyes that swallowed the things I saw. I never could learn how to rope.

"Make a loop and hold it, here," Howard says, moving my hand from the leather-wrapped honda to a place halfway down the droop-ing oval. "Now swing it, from your wrist, Pandy, not the elbow."

Howard stands behind me so I feel the buckle of his belt in the middle of my back. He puts his hands over mine, and moves the rope above my head. "Feel that?" he says.

The rhythm of the rope, his swinging, is in my wrist and arm, my belly even. Howard doesn't let go. "Feel that?" he asks again. We are moving with the rope, tight to each other, in tiny circles. He pulls the coiled rope tight into my chest and holds it there. I wish he would step back, and I don't know why.

There is a bucket on the ground in front of us and I want to try to rope it now, on my own. He counts to three and we are both supposed to let go at the same time, point the rope down our arms, onto the bucket. I wait half a second, let go after him. The loop caves in the air, drops shapeless and limp before the bucket.

I hear a sound, look up to see Brenda watching us from the doorway to the shack. Her blue eyes are strange, looking straight through me, through Howard, fixing on the rope.

Howard was our ranch foreman for eleven years. He and his family came when I was five. He was small and gentle with his hands, quick to flash a perfect, even smile. He knew about tagging calves and stretching barbed-wire tight, catching barn-sour ranch horses with a steady eye and piece of twine. He'd come riding up when you were so hot and bored from sitting by the dam and watching cows you wanted to cry. Somehow the water in his canteen would still be cold, or it would be ice tea with lemon and sugar when you were expecting plain water. He might wink, pull a baby rattler's button out of his pocket and show you how it worked, or unfold the cow/calf book to a drawing he had made of San Peppy, the greatest cutting horse that ever lived.

Howard replaces my father in most of my early memories. Maybe that's because while I was out learning to ride, my father was running the huge Steiger tractor from light to dark. He came home so dusty you couldn't tell his skin from his eyebrows. That's how I'll always think of farming—two water blue eyes set in a face the color of dirt. He once rode horses, but I never saw him up on one. Only a picture where he's standing beside a wiry buckskin named Woody, holding the thin leather reins between two fingers, like something hot. My sister framed that photo, set it on the mantel so everyone can see him with two good legs, standing beside the dust brown horse that died before I was born.

My father let Brenda and Howard and me take care of the cattle and the haying, and the real ranch chores like saddling a hairy, winter-rank horse and riding out back in the trees to check the calving cows.

When Brenda started getting too busy with track and rodeo club and swing choir, all those high school activities that keep a country girl in town until after dark, Howard started taking me along instead. His hands were always gentle with a nervous heifer or a yearling filly with a wire cut. Later, in a corner of the tack room, or while I was sliding off my horse, anytime my back was turned or I couldn't slip away, his hands were gentle with me, too.

~ ~ ~

I don't see the weasel for a week, then suddenly there are three of them, all red wire and glow.

"They're so tame," Brenda is whispering, right into my ear. "Like house cats!" Seeing, she believes me.

"They're common weasels," I tell her, having looked them up in the encyclopedia last night. She rolls her eyes. Already knew.

Two of the weasels are small, dusty red colored. They seem shy, with tiny, clever hands. They hang back by the chute. The other is bolder, my old friend I think, and he comes right up to smell my pants leg. I know better than to try to touch him, but I reach out anyway, stopping short when he rises to full, hind-leg height and scolds. *Chiff! Chiff!* He takes a step closer. *Chiff!*

"Be careful," Brenda says, backing just a step. "They could have diseases." She kneels down though and looks him right in the eye. I can tell she thinks he's beautiful, too.

We sit watching the weasels, our horses caught and not yet saddled. Monty walks by leading his scrawny gelding, Buck. He's looking at the weasels, too, pretending to be taking a long time checking one of Buck's front legs.

Now even Cal has to admit the weasels exist. But he walks by without stopping or looking down, his mouth twisted into something cruel beneath his great, hooked nose.

"You girls get to work," he yells from inside the shack. "Day's wasting."

"Yeah, girls. Get to work," Monty mutters as he swings his saddle up.

Brenda shoots him a look that says, "I'll take it from Cal, but not from you." But she jumps up anyway to saddle Bonnie, and the weasels scatter.

Howard's sons worked as hard as anyone when someone was watching but liked to goof off when only Brenda and I were around. Monty was fourteen, a year older than Brenda. He was thick, with a square face and wiry blond curls. He rarely spoke to me, but sometimes when Brenda's school friends came out for a ride, he would chase those older girls, giggling, into the dam.

Shane made my skin crawl. He was coarse with muscle and incredibly strong for his age. Just three years older than I, he could throw bales right into place at the top of the stack, wrassle the biggest bull calves at branding time.

His face was oddly girl-like though, with thick pouting lips and a dimple in his chin. He would watch me when no one was around with strangely empty eyes.

I hated him and was fascinated, all at once. He paid attention to me, cruel attention, but sometimes that was enough. Some days I fluttered around him the way a moth batters itself against a night-light. Other days he terrified me.

Shane didn't seem to care much, one way or the other, about horses, but they sure didn't like him. Lightning raced in circles around the pen, raising clouds of dust you could see from the next pasture over, whenever Shane tried to catch her. He didn't even try breaking colts. Howard must have seen the way the two-year-olds snorted away from him when he was pouring oats. Like they smelled something not quite right. Somehow the rabbits weren't afraid of him, though. Maybe they were just stupid, because they didn't seem to mind when the guys caught and butchered them. They waited patiently to be picked up by the hocks, swung at a post, then carried over the dam grade to be gutted.

One time the sandy-colored doe Shane started to clean wasn't quite dead. She screamed when he slit her belly, then bucked and kicked out of his hands and down the hill, trailing lumpy strings of intestines. Shane made a big deal of stalking, then pouncing on her at the bottom.

Shane wasn't much of a roper either, when I look back on it. I remember him almost taking his pinkie off when he dallied on to a cancer-eye cow and caught his hand between the rope and saddle horn. His finger was purple and bleeding from the rope burns, and he hunched over on his mare, Peaches, holding his hand to his belly, letting the cow run off with his rope.

I see him, frozen there like that against a clear blue sky. There was blood rubbed off on his other hand and shirtsleeve. I remember staring at him, watching him bite his thick bottom lip, stick his tongue out the corner of his mouth like a half-eaten strawberry. I remember thinking, *he looks nothing like his father.* Nothing like Howard's soft, knowing eyes, Shane's eyes were pale, angry blue, and empty as the bubbles in river ice.

It's a little cooler here by the catfish dam, just downslope of the shack, but still must be close to a hundred degrees. Some of the cows, the black ones that get the hottest, are standing half in, half out of the dam. The others just crowd into a knot and wait for evening, swinging their heads and tails at the flies.

I see a couple of rabbits not far from the shack. One is mostly brown with white ears, a new one Cal brought up last week. The rabbit is especially sweet—dark eyes and tiny white feet. I watch him eat—nervous chewing, eyes somewhere else.

I hear laughter from the corrals. I scrabble up the pile of rotting telephone poles to check. They're taking turns roping a bucket. From here it looks like they're rattling and hurling the bucket through the air by magic, or remote control.

Roping is another one of those things Brenda is just naturally good at. I've tried but can't manage even the short, drooping kid's rope Howard gave me. He tried to teach me, but I am hopeless. Shane is improving, though. Even I can see that.

I slide back down the poles, then roll onto my side, just missing the little prickly pear on my right. From the corner of my eye I see the weasel again. He is crouched under a post near his hole, like a slim chestnut garter snake.

His eyes are fixed on a meadowlark perched on top of the post, and I see his tail twitch, like a barn cat after a mouse. His tail is tufted on the end, like a bobcat's ears, and I can see tiny whiskers bristling from the curve of his elbow. I rock forward, settling on my belly, willing the bird to escape. The meadowlark puffs yellow chest feathers, then with a nervous titter, flies away. The weasel's crackling black eyes catch mine, accusing.

After this, we started seeing the weasels nearly every day. The smaller two I never could tell apart. I named the largest one Ember, after a chestnut horse in a story I'd read. I never tired of watching him, the way he held the sun inside, sparked each time he moved. When no one was looking I actually touched Ember, let him creep up my outstretched leg. It was a secret, this touching. He wouldn't come up to anyone else.

It is noon shift—almost too hot to bear. I am poking around for weasels behind the chutes, looking for their hiding place but not finding much. Grasshoppers explode around me like firecrackers, and a locust whirs from somewhere by my feet.

Howard and Brenda are getting ready to doctor a lump-jaw cow, so I'm surprised when he walks around the corner with my horse saddled. He asks me to ride up to the dam just beyond the saddleback salt licks, about half a mile north of the corrals. I don't think to ask why I am being sent alone. I scramble up on Susie, my old mud brown Morgan mare, and ride off.

But it is so hot. Once away from the shack all hills look alike, and the horizon and sky begin to circle around and around, no beginning, no end. I am suddenly afraid. I drag Susie's head to the right, then the left. I can't find the saddleback, where two hills meet in a narrow ridge shaped like a horse's withers, with a bare spot on top where Howard drops yellow blocks of salt for the cattle. I look for those blocks, their smooth craters and whirls. The grass reaches Susie's knees and there is no break in it, no path to follow. I start to cry.

Susie drops her head to graze, rooting the reins down to the knot, which I hold in both hands. Her head is sunk, up to her tiny brown ears, in a bunch of sweet clover. We stand there like that for a few minutes; I'm glad no one can hear me cry.

Susie decides on her own that it's time to head back. She turns and walks back down the draw we must have come up. How could I not have seen? We are back at the shack in ten minutes, my face dry.

But I see Brenda's horse, Bonnie, and Lightning, Howard's mare, standing, each with a hind leg cocked, beside the shack. And Brenda and Howard are there too, sitting on the board stretched between two barrels along the chute, where we stand to pour dippers full of fly dope on the cattle's backs as they string by.

Brenda is lying back somehow in Howard's lap. His hands are searching for something inside her jeans. They jump up when I ride in. Brenda has to go loosen Bonnie's cinch right away.

"We had a bet going whether that's a one- or two-piece swimsuit she has on there under her duds," Howard says, talking fast and loud. I look over at Brenda. She has a T-shirt on, and jeans. Permed blond hair hides her eyes. "Why are you back so soon?" Howard asks.

I try to answer but no words come out. I can't say I was lost, and somehow I feel I shouldn't be back now. Even the wind has stopped blowing, and I sit in the hot and quiet, not knowing what to do.

"You're too hot, aren't you, Pandy?" he asks. "Get off and take some water."

I ride Susie right up under the tin overhang and get off in the shade. Brenda doesn't say a word to me the rest of the afternoon.

~ ~ ~

Rabbits are disappearing. Cal found a patch of white hair, soft as dandelion skin, blown against the shack this morning. We both lay down in the dust to look under the shack but can see nothing in the dark. Shane runs to find a flashlight, and we look again. Twelve eyes glow back, wide, frightened.

"Must have been the coyotes," Shane says. "That's four this week." He pinches the back of my leg and I jump, knock my head against the hitching rail getting up. Cal doesn't see.

"Ain't no coyote getting them under there," Cal says. "It's those weasels of Pandy's."

I feel a burn start low in my chest, below my heart. Something like fear. The weasels are mine, and they are killing the spotted rabbits.

Weasels kill and eat rabbits. I know this now, so I can picture what was happening up at the shack at night, that summer a long time ago.

I see the weasel is hungry. It's there in his dark eyes, and something more. An enjoyment of pain, a joy in his wild, boneless leaps. But now he is still, a shadow behind the greater shadow of a fallen fence post.

His victim is the dark brown rabbit with white ears. The rabbit is unconcerned, his little jaw viciously seesawing a blade of grass.

The weasel is stalking the rabbit who doesn't realize, doesn't run away. The weasel is creeping up, legless as a snake. His narrow head low, nose trailing the dust like a bloodhound. The white-eared rabbit sees him and is frozen, eyes blank, yet filled with his fate.

The weasel leaps and straddles the rabbit like a cowboy busting a bronc. The rabbit stiffens and screams as the weasel finds the pencil-thin bones of his neck. Wind, in from the west, carries away the rabbit's cry.

One week later I am riding back toward the shack from the pothole dam just up the hill. Shadows attach to my horse's legs and follow us home, stretching and creeping farther toward the darkness in the east.

Shane and Cal had gone back early to breed some cows, and

now I see only Shane's mare Peaches tied to the post along the shack. I wonder where Cal is, since the truck is still parked there, right up to the shack, bumper nearly touching.

I still don't see Shane as I get off Pride, and I'm hoping, somehow, that he's not here.

I turn around and plant my back against Pride's saddle, drawing the latigo over my right shoulder, then heave again and feel the buckle slip loose from leather. I pull the saddle down on top of me, my sunburned forearms prickling against Pride's sweaty back. The stirrups dangle, bumping the packed ground as I drag the saddle into the cool darkness of the shack. I hear his breathing just before the wooden door scrapes nearly shut behind me. Shane is in here with me, blocking the door, and there is no way out.

I must have dropped the saddle, backed into a corner. I don't remember being afraid, but I know I prayed Cal wouldn't come back and find us that way. I never looked at Shane. My world narrowed to the slice of prairie beyond the half-shut door. This is what I remember: Outside the sun is painting the prairie red and gold. I see the brown rabbit with white ears, frozen there between the shack and horse pen. He is crouched in the grass, silent and insignificant against the sunset. His eyes are empty and hazy as the dusty grass. I imagine a hawk circling overhead, peering through the reddish dust, diving with talons outstretched, and, without mercy, piercing his fragile hide.

~ ~ ~

There is killing, cruelty, everywhere. I used to think God watched us all the time, from somewhere in the sky. But I stopped believing, for a while, and the sky became a hollow place.

The weasels killed the rabbits. All of them I suppose. And so in the scheme of things, the rabbits were the victims, the prey. But the cruelty goes further than that.

Monty is driving the old bronze Chevy he calls Wounded Knee up over the hill from the south gate, and I'm with him in the front seat. He's telling me about a rattlesnake he thought he'd heard in their basement, only it turned out to be a fluorescent lightbulb fizzing out. We stop at the shack beside the ranch's gray diesel Cal and Howard drove up for the noon shift. He's still talking. There is something on the hood of the diesel that I don't recognize at first. My door creaks open and I get out.

There are three weasels stretched out on a brown saddle blanket. My mouth is dry. Three weasels, one bigger, red as the setting sun. Two that look alike, mouths dragged sideways in snarl. They were shot, all three, through the head, their narrow bellies, and chests. They lie still on the hood of the truck in a way life never can, gathering what's left of the sun in their glowing fur.

There is no way to describe how still the weasels lay in that sun. I stood there a long time, with the heat rising from the truck's ugly metal hood into my face. Cal and Shane stood around laughing, telling the killing of those weasels like a giant joke. Howard wasn't in sight, so Shane picked up one of the dead weasels and danced with it, tried to drape it over my shoulder. It was Ember. I backed away from him and fell over a rotted fence post. The men laughed.

When I got up, Shane was back by the pickup and I watched him throw Ember back down on the blanket. I saw him pull his knife from out of his front pocket and start skinning. I watched his wide back and shit-spattered jeans, the way he stood with his legs planted apart and shoulders thrown back. I knew the smell of greasy hair under his Michelin tire cap, the way his thick hands felt on my neck, and inside my clothes. I tried to hate him. But everything was cold inside, and hollow, and my eyes kept coming back to the saddle blankets on the hood of that truck.

~ ~ ~

I have taken a long time to realize that a cowboy who is gentle with a nervous colt or quick to stand up in church to lead a prayer may not be the man everyone imagines him to be. Shane was rough and cruel already at twelve, thirteen, fourteen, and easy for me to blame. Howard was something different. None of what I'd been taught about good and evil seemed to apply.

I coped the only way I could. I learned to look sideways at things, leaving room for explanations, doubts. I felt uneasy when Howard would show up in the big Ford diesel to pick me up after school or a basketball game, but I couldn't say why. So I would get in, sit tensed against the door handle, waiting, never thinking to just get out.

I knew something was wrong, terribly wrong, when he pinned me up against the rabbit cages and kissed me—my first kiss—so hard my mouth bled. But afterward I wasn't sure who to tell, or if I'd done something wrong, or if anything had really happened at all. The next day he was gentle again. The Smith kids came down to help us work the cattle, and Howard was everywhere at once, helping someone run the headgate, teaching Brenda to throw a fancy loop, showing me the difference between pigeon-toed and splay-footed in a pen of ranch horses. When we were alone for a second he whispered in my ear that I was the best horseman of the bunch, had the best eye, the best seat. He smiled down at me the way a perfect father might. I learned to close off what I was thinking, what I may have remembered. I learned not to see.

I still can't quite see Howard's face the way it was when he was touching me. I see him on the back of blaze-faced Gem, smiling, teeth perfect, even. Kneeling to pull a prairie flower from the soil and show me how the roots work to gather moisture. For the rest, my eyes were closed. You can tear a child's voice away as naturally as an animal gnaws and consumes flesh.

Raised in a family that avoided painful topics, by parents who couldn't even whisper certain facts of life, my sister and I were easy prey, sure to keep our silence.

In the end, it was Brenda who broke the silence. Seven years after this summer of weasels and rabbits, Brenda told my parents about Howard and his sons. Later she said she did it for me, because she knew what must be happening and couldn't stay silent any longer. And so his family packed and moved away, all in a month. My father didn't want to make a fuss; no one but our family and the pastor knew. That was still too many for me.

Everyone blamed my father for firing such a faithful foreman. Even my English teacher, Mrs. Powers, spent ten minutes on the first day of class that fall explaining that our schoolmate, Howard's daughter, Joan, would not be returning this fall. How some people fired their employees for no reason, threw them and their children out into the street. Her words, her small, gray eyes, were nails punching through my skin.

I'm sure there was more talk. I've heard whispers that our church was in an uproar that whole summer, for Howard was a deacon and everyone took sides. I don't remember that. In the end, I simply refused to talk about it, and no one really asked. I wore the inside of my mouth raw, rode out every night to check the cows and came home after dark.

I was sixteen when he went away. I don't remember his actual leaving. In fact, I don't remember much from that time. There are blank days and months and years, no matter how hard I try. Instead, I go back to the summer I turned nine. I remember the weasels and rabbits.

After Howard and Shane left, I learned to break a colt all by myself, with kindness and a snaffle instead of a curb. I stopped killing rattlesnakes for no reason and began to listen when the coyotes cried. I may still learn to rope.

Stories are never really finished, though. There are memories that hide behind words. They come to me, unexpected, in the sweet smell of sweaty saddle blankets, or the sound of footsteps from a darkened hall. I break into a sweat if someone follows me into a room without another door. My heart pounds and I am afraid to turn around, afraid not to. I am in that moment, with the weasels lying dead under broken sky, and that moment never fades.

THE DIFFERENCES BETWEEN

To most people, all the prairie, from Pipestone, Minnesota, to the first rolling shadows of the Black Hills, looks the same. Fields drift into pastures, one farmhouse becomes twenty, a thousand tractors blow dust from a thousand black-dirt fields, until Dakota is all one sun-bleached blur. One town is like any other, and the men in jeans and scuffed brown boots all seem the same.

From the road, the towns, too, look much the same. One exit sign and half a dozen billboards for the two cafés in town, a dog sleeping on the Sinclair station's concrete porch. A water tower with the town's name painted in big black letters, so no one living there forgets.

But the people who live in these small towns notice differences. About everything and everyone. Differences split communities, families, down the middle sometimes, perhaps for generations.

There's a lot of flat land and sky between the people who live in Murdo and those in the next town. People use this space to make divisions: locals versus tourists; east-river towns compared to west; town kids against country kids; believers versus unbelievers; Daums as compared to Baughmans; and especially, cattlemen as opposed to farmers.

DAUMS AND BAUGHMANS

Like the Hatfields and McCoys, Okaton's Daums and Baughmans (pronounced bog-mahn) have been farming and feuding, side by side, for generations. This quarrel would be less noticeable in a larger town, but Okaton is home to only three families that are neither Daum nor Baughman.

It's safe to say that any farmer seen on his tractor or in his truck within a twelve-mile radius is either a Baughman or a Daum. Stop and talk to him for five minutes and you'll probably guess which one he is without asking.

Both the Daums and Baughmans come from tough, Bible-minded Dutch stock. The families came over at roughly the same time, around 1910. They settled in Okaton because the ground was fertile and cheap and just as flat as the fields they remembered back home. Both families worked the ground and raised great broods of children. The similarities pretty much end there, though.

Where the early Daums were short, stout, and cheerful, the Baughmans shot up thin and angular, silent as fence posts. To this day, my mother names the tallest stalks of sorghum in our front field, the ones that poke up a foot above the rest, "Alberts." This after Albert Baughman, 6'8".

"Just look at that," she says on a good year, when the sorghum has billowed up to seven feet tall. She's pointing to a giant, tasseled stalk. "That one's an Albert in a whole field of Baughmans."

And it's not just size. The Daums are talkers. Anything related to weather, football, or religion is fair game. They crowd in knots after church and during family reunions, rehashing Mark Daum's stint with the Nebraska Cornhuskers, Darrel Daum's wheat blight.

"Steiger'sradiatorbroke," my dad's brother Gerry says. "GottafixitMondaymorning."

My Uncle Pete is talking at the same time. "Burntheengineoutthatway." Their voices blend into the staccato tapping of a single snare drum. "Whataboutthatnorthfield?"

My father joins in. "Wheat'saboutreadytoharvest. Mightstormtomorrow." They understand each other perfectly. Pete is the slowest of the three, but he makes up for lost time by repeating "Amen" and "Praise the Lord!" at every opportunity.

Pete is an exemplary Daum—a truck-driving farmer who is protected by the hand of God. You wouldn't know that by looking at him. He's short and always smiling, still combs his hair back in a shining, silver wave. He has permanent half-moons of grease under all his fingernails, talks twice as fast as anyone but a Daum can listen.

He has picked up numerous hitchhikers and introduced them to Jesus. Some were carrying knives and had hurt or killed someone in the past. I picture him in the cab of his old semi, thick hands working the gears, a beatific smile on his round, glowing face. He's humming a magnificent rendition of "Amazing Grace" to the escaped convict sitting to his right.

"Do you know Jesus?" Pete asks.

The grizzled convict slumps into a confused puddle of stinking leather jacket and shifting eyes. "Never met him," he grunts.

"Well, let me tell you about my sweetest friend," Pete continues. While he's talking, an eight-track tape rolls out the soul-stirring melodies of the Bill Gaither Trio.

The convict sits for hours, dazed. He promises to talk to Jesus every night. He and Pete pray together before parting ways at the next diesel stop. As Pete pulls away, the convict blinks a few times and shakes his head. The spell is broken.

We all hold our breath when Pete is hauling hay or on an interstate run. Once he rolled his pickup down an eighty-foot embankment. He wasn't wearing a seat belt, and had a broken TV set on the seat beside him. The pickup rolled three times and landed on its tires. Pete sat there for a minute just holding the steering wheel and praying. He wasn't sure he was still alive and wondered even more when the pickup started on the first try. His pickup never started on the first try. He drove it out the pasture gate, engine humming. The TV worked when he plugged it in that night. None of us were surprised. God loves Pete. He's a Daum.

No Baughman would pick up convict hitchhikers or expect the grace of God to heal a television set. Baughmans speak mostly in silences. At a Baughman family reunion there are long pauses, soul-excavating stares. To hear a conversation between a Daum and Baughman is to hear a lot of Daum.

The Okaton church itself is split cleanly down its narrow central aisle. Daums sit on hard, wooden pews on the east side of the church, Baughmans tower a head or two above them on equally hard wooden pews to the west. There is a plain wooden table in the front, and a raised pulpit, which is the only place in the church where the pastor can stand taller than a Baughman.

There are a few rebels. Bachelor men, no matter what their kin, sit east side, in the back. My Uncle Pete arrives five minutes late most Sunday mornings, and so he and Flora alternate, depending on which side has space.

You have to understand that this is a tiny church. Thirty people attend on a good Sunday, and half of those are children under twelve. There is only one family that is neither Daum nor Baughman, and since they are a tall and bony lot, they sit precariously on the west side, honorary Baughmans.

I've seen tall, stern-eyed Marvin Baughman surveying his crop of sons when I walk into the room. Two of them are horse crazy, like me, and are finding ways to make a living breaking colts and roping calves for one hundred dollars a day at other ranchers' brandings. Marvin must think I'm a bad influence.

Women in Okaton are traditionally their husbands' helpmates. This tradition, unfortunately, includes the Daums. Daughters are expected to marry a Christian man, raise children, cook supper, and help with chores, but not run businesses alone. I don't fit in.

Marvin Baughman mostly doesn't like the way I look into the dusty corners of our religion; he doesn't like the way I ask questions that can't have any answers. He hates the way I talk and laugh and wear Doc Martens inside the church. It doesn't seem right to him that I breed show horses for a living. He doesn't want me or my horses getting too close to all his bachelor sons.

He doesn't have to worry. There have been feuds and a few friendships, but never a marriage between a Baughman and a Daum. There are simply too many differences. I could never measure up, and wouldn't want to.

Most Baughmans are valedictorians of their classes. They play basketball with the need to win and can run a Daum kid into dust at local track meets. But they don't seem to have much fun. That's a Daum's eye view of things at least.

THOSE WHO STAY AND THOSE WHO GO

The winds that blow prairie grasses flat from the root push hard against the people and buildings of Murdo, South Dakota, too. Some days, the sun itself seems to blow right outside the horizon, and clouds move so fast you can't catch their shadow with a stepped-up Chevy.

Women learn to hold their skirts between their knees and children grow up leaning. Years later, those who end up staying walk down Main Street on calm days leaning from the waist, facing an imaginary wind.

There are four paved streets in Murdo. One blinking traffic light. Not much to tempt high school graduates to stay.

Kids can work at the truck stop, waiting tables, pumping gas, or washing dishes, through high school and beyond. There are four other gas stations in town. There is the Super-Valu market. The Tee-Pee and Star restaurants. The Pioneer Auto Museum and Hallmark gift shop. There is a feed store attached to the grain elevator. The soil conservation building, post office, West River Electric Company, a telephone repair service, one plumber. The Silver Grill café, the high school and grade school, a public library open only on Thursday afternoons. The Blue Bison bar and four hotels. There is hourly work driving tractors and bucking hay bales every summer, sometimes a job watching pregnant heifers all night long during spring calving.

A lot of kids move off to Sioux Falls or Rapid City, where there are jobs. Some go as far as Omaha or Minneapolis, others go farther. These are the ones who leave, and they are recognized as such early on.

Don't ask me how people know. I knew. I could run a finger down the pictures in the high school yearbook, picking who would stay and who would go.

We hear about the ones who go in bits and pieces. They're mentioned now and then in Bernice Baughman's newspaper, the *Coyote*. There's a scholarship announcement here, a birth announcement there. But these kids who leave drift from people's thoughts and fade away, until they return for a visit, and people stare low and long and hard, as if trying to make out a particularly grainy picture. No one's sure what to say. These kids have stepped over an invisible line, and are never seen quite the same way.

For those who stay, the nights start getting long. There's no question about having children. Everyone does if they can, if for no other reason than to break the silence of those winter nights. There is joy as well, though not the kind most people expect. Joy comes in small, daily pleasures. The incredible colors of the sunsets here. Watching your son win a buckle at a 4-H rodeo. Neighbors helping your husband harvest wheat when he's laid up for a week with kidney stones. I could go on.

I've mentioned the jobs people who stay might have. There are other things to do. Church twice on Sundays, Wednesday nights, more days if you can think of reasons. Study groups. Men's prayer breakfasts. Ladies aid.

There are spring banquets, father and son dinners, Book-and-Thimble Club readings, the Lion's Club raffles. The grade school Christmas concert. Gideon meetings, where men hand out stacks of Bibles, hold hands in a circle to pray. There are pool tables, and enough bottles of beer to make you forget your day, your week, maybe even a whole year, at the Blue Bison bar.

In between, though, are days stretching longer than an empty country road. Those who stay learn early: this is a flat and sparsely peopled land. There will be few travelers and fewer friends. Loneliness is just another disease here. Its symptoms are sicknesses, too. Depression. Alcoholism. Parochialism. Suicide.

Some winter nights people crowd in to watch high school basketball in the sweltering auditorium. Everyone comes to watch, sweat, and munch burned popcorn, whether they have a boy playing or not. Down vests and waterproof parkas spill out of the coatroom, where they're nestled three to a hanger. School kids sit at the west end of the bleachers, girls lean back between the boys' legs. Fat girls, and girls with pimples, sit alone. Outside, stars glitter like holes punched in the blackest cloth. The cold is still and burning.

I'm a somewhere-in-between. I've been gone so much, most people consider me a leaver. But I run a business from our family ranch and haven't missed a summer's worth of ranch work since I could walk and shinny up a horse. It's true I've spent most of the last three winters in Colorado, finishing graduate school, and five winters before that working on my undergraduate degree. But all along I was building up my broodmare herd, waiting for the day I would come back home. I have built my business and my life around a four-thousand-acre square of prairie, and no matter how far I travel, that will always be my home.

Even so, I don't really belong. After eight years of college, I am a stranger in my hometown. Jackie Schwartz, who was one grade ahead of me in school, looks at my shoes whenever I walk into the hardware store where she works.

I remember sitting with her in the attic of the auditorium, where the band stores its tubas and bass drums and music stands. Jackie and I watched the basketball games from up there, leaning over a flimsy balcony rail, occasionally daring our stomachs to settle in our shoes by leaning just a bit too far.

It seemed we knew before anybody in the stands whether

the ball would sink through the basket, whether the complicated zone defense was working. We giggled at our view of couples in the student section of the stands—whose hands were where, under whose sweater. And we both felt safe telling our secrets there.

"I feel like God up here," Jackie told me once. "It's the only place I can look down on everyone else, but no one's watching me. No one can get at me here."

I knew Jackie sometimes came to school with purple bruises behind her freckles, but I never asked her why. That wasn't something we talked about when I was growing up. No one in Murdo did.

After Jackie said that, the basketball game still went on below, but it seemed silly somehow. As if we could see the pattern of it all, how the game would turn out, just by watching from this height. From where we stood, the plays really did look like the arrows and semicircles and curving lines we'd seen on Coach Wheeler's board. It was all so simple. When the smell of sweat and popcorn finally reached us, at the end of the second half, it was time to go home.

Now we're both adults, and she observes me carefully, from a distance of two arms' lengths, as she's writing up my ticket. Her hair is pulled back in a ponytail with bangs, just the way she wore it in school. She has two boys of her own now, both blond and bucktoothed and freckled like their mother. I've seen them at the Dairy Freeze on summer nights, along with her red-headed husband, Jerry Smith. He was a senior back in our days of balcony watching. One of those boys who always had a freshman or sophomore girl leaning back into his lap, his hands always hidden in the woolen folds of her jacket.

"How's it going?" I ask. "Had any rain out your way?"

She looks up at me, face freckled from the sun. "Nope. Been dry." She looks back down. I think I see bruising under her eyes, fragile, the color of the sky.

I nod and take my receipt, not knowing what to say. We are strangers now, seeing the world from our different places.

In other towns I am also a stranger. I stop along a busy street, somewhere far from South Dakota, to search the sky for dark clouds piling on the horizon, wonder at the chance for rain. My fleeting thoughts: Are the horses in? Ranch trucks protected from the hail? Tomatoes covered?

It's more than this. Somehow I don't belong anywhere but inside myself, and sometimes even there I'm restless. What keeps me in South Dakota?

Horses looking up from their graze as I walk by. Clouds moving across the sun. The grass that holds the prairie dirt. Thirsty roots sunk deep.

BELIEVERS AND UNBELIEVERS

Nearly all of Murdo's 697 inhabitants are going to heaven. Keeping this idea firmly in mind, they can ignore the dust storm blowing topsoil down Lincoln Street from the wheat fields north of town. They can be thankful for the four paved streets in town, the flashing red light put in at the four-way stop down by the Triple H truck stop.

For those who live outside of Murdo, on the ranches and farms scattered around the tiny town of Okaton, heaven can seem both near and far. This winter it is far from here, from central South Dakota, from the Great Plains, and, after the re-election of President Clinton, from the nation in general. Heaven is certainly far from all this snow, from the blizzard winds and rain curling down as ice.

Okaton's tiny, one-room church rises up out of the plains, a squat box made of cement and wood. There is no steeple or cross, nothing to tell the motorists racing by on Interstate 90 that God lives here, in a lot backed by woolly faced Hereford cattle and Hattie Vanderkamp's well-ordered vegetable patch.

Someone planted a few spindly trees out front, and there is a thinly wooded shelterbelt between the church and Vanderkamp's house. But other than that, the church is bare to the winds blowing out of the north and east, to the snow that wraps around the block corners of the foundations and won't let go.

On Sunday mornings the gravel parking lot is packed with more four-wheel drive pickups and family-size sedans than there are people in Okaton, because farmers and ranchers drive twelve miles down bare dirt roads to come to this church. They leave their broken water pumps and smooth-handled fencing pliers, the John Deere tractor parked out by the shop, all four giant tires lined up straight and square. The cattle are fed early and ranch horses snooze by round bale feeders. This is a day of rest.

The God preached from this church's bare wood pulpit twenty years ago might have been one Luther and Calvin and a few other old-timers would have recognized. The message since then has been softened by a succession of pastors shared with the Evangelical Free Church in Murdo. It's hard to find a pastor for a Dutch Reformed church with thirty worshipers, counting babies, on any good Sunday. So now the message is laced with love and kindness, and there are fewer references to the fires of hell. The congregation as a whole, while still saved, smiles more.

Each Sunday school class is separated by a sheet hung as a curtain, or maybe by a chalkboard, as it was when I was a child. We all thought that everyone inside this church, or at least in this curtained room, must be a believer. The others were outside, hunched in the cars roaring down the interstate, sitting on stools in the Blue Bison bar. They were cussing as they waited in line at drive-thrus, hitting their dogs with fists as big around as bowls. We prayed for them at night.

I was taught to pity unbelievers, to be an example to the non-Christian but not too close a friend. I was taught not to date or marry an unbeliever, not to be "unequally yoked," as the pastor would say.

My Christian friends and I really were different from the other kids. We knew we were being watched. God was the threat lurking under all good fun, the eyes watching when no one else could see. Unblinking. All day he watched, waiting for mistakes. The sun was his eye. And he always caught up to me at night. He waited for me to climb into bed, then breathed questions in my ear: "Why did you say that to your sister? Did you hurt your mother's feelings after dinner? What would I have done?"

How could you explain this guilt, the being watched and not quite measuring up, to an unbeliever? What would we have in common? It never occurred to me that children in Pierre or Wall or even Murdo who were unbelievers could think like me.

Salvation was what marked the difference—like a seal stamped on all our foreheads. This is the way I understood life, back in the cold basement Sunday school room of the Okaton church. The way Daum and Baughman kids are still understanding it today. Life was black and white, lines drawn in the sand. You were either saved or unsaved. You were going to heaven or hell. There were believers and unbelievers.

CATTLEMEN AND FARMERS

The difference between cattlemen and farmers goes way back. It started something like this:

> Now Abel was a keeper of sheep, but Cain was a tiller
> of the ground.
>> —Genesis 4:2

My family and our ranch are something in between. My sister and I are cattlemen, our father a farmer. The land itself is neither east nor west—torn between land best used for cattle and sheep, or corn and dryland wheat.

We straddle South Dakota's east-west split between farm

and grassland. Most of the landowners around Murdo and Okaton focus on farming, running a small herd of black white-faced cows to graze the land not fit for wheat or alfalfa. Just west of us, around Kadoka, few acres are plowed for dryland wheat, and the herds of cattle and horses keep getting bigger, the range more open, all the way west to the Black Hills.

I noticed early the differences between cattlemen and farmers. Those differences seemed as blatant as the four-wire fence separating old man Pruitt's land from ours. The quiet, gray-eyed Okaton farmers wore sober western suits and ties every Sunday at the Dutch Reformed church. The leather-skinned cattle ranchers chewed tobacco, swore out loud, and served ice-cold beer at spring brandings. The two groups rarely mixed.

My father owns a ranch, but first and foremost he is a farmer, and therefore a son of Cain.

The Daums have always been farmers, men who turned the earth, who toiled and waited and watched, who found something precious buried there. And they were all church-going men. There are pastors and missionaries scattered like blackbirds throughout our family tree.

My grandfather died young, but all forty years his hands were caked with dust when he'd fold them for the evening prayer. My father has five brothers. Ned, Pete, Nick, Gerry, Dick. All except Ned, the oldest, walk heavy and low to the earth. They are strong men, with round chests and thick legs, like heavy roots. They bristle with whiskers, except on

Sundays, and sometimes scrape the dirt off their pant legs before walking into the house. I've heard every one of them pray out loud before a meal, thanking God for the gifts he's given, or that he's about to bestow.

All this worship trickled down as I was growing up, so that I was supposed to know God was linked to the land itself. God knew Dad had planted corn yesterday and would consider those hopeful, yellow grains when he planned the monthly rains.

Just as he grew up praying, my father grew up working in the fields. He rode horses, sure enough, but they were mutton-withered workhorses straight off the plow, and his saddle was a folded cloth. Later he would buy a herd of black white-faced cows with Ned and Pete, and under my father's management, this herd became one of the best in the state. So he was a cattleman, too. But when it came down to it, he was still all farmer. Thick and strong, short, bristling as a root. Even when he walked, he looked down. He wore overalls out to the feed shed, loved working the machinery that carried damp, caramel brown silage to the bunks where the calves ate.

I remember walking out to find him one winter afternoon when I was seven years old. The shed roared, dust swirled so thick inside I covered my mouth with one cupped palm so it wouldn't coat my teeth. The machinery ground and throbbed inside my throat. The noise was like screaming with someone else's voice.

I saw my father as a shadow through the dust. He had his hands cupped up to his face, like he was crying. I walked slowly, not sure, until I could see.

His gloves were full of silage—a thick brown cone pressed up to his nose like a flower. He was breathing it in, maybe tasting it, too. I couldn't tell.

He didn't see me. I screamed, "Telephone!"

He looked up, face powdered nearly white from corn dust. His eyes were somewhere else, and they came slowly back. For a moment he stood there with that palm full of silage held up like an offering, to me or to God. Then he dropped it and disappeared into the dust to shut the silo down. I crouched down near the front of the conveyer, where he'd been standing. There was a pile of spilled silage up over my ankles. I took a handful up to my nose.

It smelled warm and sweet, but sour, too, like pickled cabbage, or milk a day from going bad. I could smell the loam, the rooted soil where it had grown.

The calves crowded around the bunks in a hairy black mass, inches from where I stood. Their breath was sweet, too, carried up like clouds from inside the bunks. My father fed them from what he'd grown, and they ate with loving, desperate concentration; they would grow and become, themselves, more food.

Cursed is the ground because of you; in toil you shall eat of it all the days of your life; thorns and thistles it shall bring forth to you; and you shall eat the plants of the field. In the sweat of your face you shall eat bread.

—Genesis 3:17–19

When I was young my father tilled the ground, all day and into the night during planting season. He smelled of dust and sweat both. This was not an easy life.

The whole world was wrapped inside his fields. He rejoiced with the rain and smelled thunderstorms days before they would arrive. Even the prospect of hail excited him. The sky was his future, for the fields were made from it. The ground was always hungry back then, until it soaked in rain like manna.

God rarely rained his blessings on my father's crops, but we were all supposed to keep praying. My father said grace before every meal, usually a request for rain and a blessing for the food. Sometimes the prayers would stretch to include the family's health and safety, and then other, more distant relations' safety, the missionaries we supported in Indonesia, and on to the individual crops of wheat and corn and oats. It could go on and on, and I'd start to wiggle, kick Brenda in the knee, or reach under the table to feed the dog pieces of roast beef straight off the platter. I knew God was watching, but I doubted that he heard every one of those prayers. Where would he get the time?

Wind and weather were at the center of the household. The sky followed my father with its naked, staring eye. Sometimes storms blew in and teased him with rain clouds. Mostly, that rain never fell. When the clouds did open up, there was a wild, sinful wash of water. Farmers watched their fields swirl south with the foaming rush of waters.

A farmer sees the clouds come in and hopes for rain. If rain comes, he parks the tractors and sits it out. He can't work a field that's wet, so he just watches that rain soak into the hot, black ground, his wheat push up hard into the sky.

Farmers are hopeful. They have no control over the rains that nourish crops. They learn to pray, to watch storm clouds moving over and through, eyes dark with distant longing.

Farmers didn't always rely on prayer alone for rain, though. From the 1950s to the mid-1970s, South Dakota experimented with cloud seeding. Men in airplanes flew close to a likely looking cloud, then sprinkled frozen nitrogen or salt pellets from the windows of the plane. The process seemed to be working—until one afternoon in June of 1972. After a minor seeding expedition, a cloud opened up over Rapid City. It rained fifteen inches in six hours. Two hundred and thirty-six people died and nearly three thousand were injured. Damages exceeded 150 million dollars. After that, though an investigation showed the cloud seeders couldn't have been at fault, the public support for cloud seeding sagged, and the planes stopped flying.

My father still looks up at the sky sometimes and wonders, out loud, what might have been if cloud seeding had been allowed to continue. I keep quiet, thankful in a way that those men failed. For what would happen to the prairie if there were always enough rain for crops? More and more land would be plowed under into neat little grids of corn and wheat. The open prairie would disappear, and with it, like the buffalo before him, would go the cattleman.

~ ~ ~

In the course of time Cain brought to the Lord an offering of the fruit of the ground, and Abel brought of the firstlings of his flock and of their fat portions. And the Lord had regard for Abel and his offering, but for Cain and his offering he had no regard.

—Genesis 4:3–5

Is it still the cattlemen who please God most? Cattlemen are God's daily ushers of birth and death. They have the power to spill living blood. While the farmer must stay out of a muddied field until it dries, the cattleman goes right back out into the newly wet world. He knows the bitter smell of lightning about to strike again, the wet green scent of sage. He teaches a green-broke colt about the rattle of rain on a brittle, yellow slicker; feels his gloves swell thick with wet. He talks to God most every day but sees little need for formal prayer.

Cattlemen carry their future over the front of their saddles, draped like a newborn calf brought in before a blizzard. How could even God do as much as the rancher, who holds so many lives in his wind-chapped hands?

There is a practical hardness about a cattleman. He knows that rain comes and goes, grass will grow up green around his cattle's hocks, or it will wither down to dust. He, too, watches the weather, but mainly in the spring, when a blizzard could wipe out a hundred newborn calves. And then he's watching from inside the barn, ready to saddle a wool-coated bronc and get his cows and calves down into a stand of trees, or up against a windbreak, where they'll have a chance.

Summer rains come and go, dust blows, or draws turn to clouded creeks that horses refuse to jump. But these are things a man can handle. I learned young that three hard smacks from the balled end of a rope and a horse will jump runoff creeks, all right. No asking God for help, no waiting for the rain to stop. Just whip the horse, and you'll go—straight up and no cushion coming down, hooves sliding in the muck, muddied water splashed up to your horse's belly. That's what rain meant to me. That and the sweet green of growing grass.

It's not that growing up I didn't respect my father. I loved his plans and childlike enthusiasm for a new idea. But when he and my mother went for a drive to see the wheat ripening in the fields up north, I stayed home.

I loved to walk on grassland instead, to kneel down to breathe on touch-me-nots growing on the bare shale slopes, to walk through wheat grass to my knees. I knew the sweet breath of horses grazing open places, the hot, dry wind that blows forever, where there is always one more blackbird on the top strand of a barbed-wire fence. I'd see whole clouds of blackbirds rising from the flooded corner of the horse pasture. Cattails growing there, and an endless sea of grass. Nothing planted.

When a meadowlark sings from its lonely perch, it is the psalmist David's voice I hear. A litany in praise of wild things and open spaces. I can get off my horse and sit down in a cathedral of grass and vaulted sky. Here I can talk to God. And the living silence is his reply.

My sister and I were the cattlemen. We rode out there,

in the rain, tasting it with our own sharp breath. There was always another creek to jump, and more grassland on the other side.

~ ~ ~

> Cain said to Abel his brother, "Let us go out to the field." And when they were in the field, Cain rose up against his brother Abel, and killed him. . . . And the Lord said, "What have you done? The voice of your brother's blood is crying to me from the ground. And now you are cursed from the ground, which has opened its mouth to receive your brother's blood from your hand. When you till the ground, it shall no longer yield to you its strength."
>
> —Genesis 4:8–12

I grew up knowing that for farmers, God is testing, always. He sends locusts and soil-ripping floods, cutworms and corn blight, a January so cold it burns winter wheat to yellow. Farmers count on pesticides or miracles. For those who don't crop dust, each day, each ear of corn, granaries full of their golden stores of wheat, are small miracles. Almost everyone uses poison to supplement his prayers.

It is always Egypt for the farmers of the plains. The '90s have brought many to their knees with its droughts and pestilence and swarms of grasshoppers, its falling price of wheat. Joseph with his coat of many colors, his stockpiles of wheat, which saved Egypt from seven years of famine, couldn't know what these stores of wheat mean to a South Dakota man. The sweat and the bills and the blood that soaks into the ground feed the precious roots of planted crops. And when the harvest comes, on that rare good year, could even a pharaoh's dreams of riches and famine reveal such perfect wealth?

Abel's loss is with us still. Farmers are still offering up their sweet green gifts, feeding God spoonfuls of dust with every prayer. They send thanksgivings for every drop of rain. And somehow, they are still rejected—by the soil for not nurturing the farmer's seeds, by the sky as it withholds its rain, by the market as it offers the same price for wheat as it did in 1950, though the cost of growing it has tripled. As always, God loves Abel best.

But to confound both, there are plagues for farmers and cattlemen alike. Perhaps this is what finally draws us together: grasshoppers that eat the corn and the grass and the leaves from the trees. The rivers running brown with badlands silt, clogged bank to bank with fallen trees and the sharp, broken parts of bridges. Firstborn sons who die before their time.

Years our prayers go unanswered we are naked, the fields ripening with empty husks instead of wheat, with gnawed and toothless ears of corn. Silage is ground from corn stalks, without the ears, and no cattle fatten well these winters. Both the cattlemen and farmers lose. Some move away for good.

God takes from cattlemen and farmers. From the town kid whose father lost his job, and from the country kid who lost his home to a farm sale. From those who worship him and from those who don't. Sometimes we Dakotans forget this in our prayers, after a day spent in the open with only the hot sun as companion. It's no wonder people become insular, start drawing lines where there were none. If people live here long enough, the sun can shrink their eyes down inside their faces, and the world itself grows small.

Seen from the window of an airplane, the shape of all things changes, merges. Fence lines vanish into the sweep of hillsides, forests gather into shadows, and there is no such thing as boundaries between counties, states, or countries. Seen from a distance, there are hardly any differences between.

WHY WE RETURN—
THE PRAIRIE IN HER EYES

Some people spend a lifetime looking back, returning again and again to words and people and places that are gone.

Three summers ago a woman, seventy years or more, came here to see what she'd missed.

She is looking out the passenger window of her silver Lincoln Continental when I step up to the car, and I notice that her eyes seem a little far away. She doesn't fit here. Her blouse is made of silk or some other shiny fabric, with alternating stripes of candy pink and fuchsia. Her face is soft and kind, and her gray eyes peer eagerly from behind big pale glasses. The driver, who may have been her son, is pale and blond and too well dressed to step into the prairie wind without rumpling. He stays in the car while his mother gets out. He drums his fingers on the steering wheel, looking bored.

"This was my father's land," she says, her voice trembling. "I'm Gertie Bishop."

Her parents homesteaded a section of rough prairie on the western edge of what is now my father's land.

"I'm glad you came," I say, meaning it. I want to watch her face when she steps out onto the prairie. See if she remembers this place, if there's some mark I might recognize in myself burned into her soul.

My father and I drive her to the site of her parents' homestead. Past the trout dam, past the yearlings massed on the far hillside, bunched up against the deer flies and relentless sun. My father is telling stories all the time, of other homesteaders whose children have returned to see the land. There haven't been many, to tell the truth.

I notice Gertie getting quiet as we stop the truck. I wish my father would stop talking. She is facing the window, but doesn't know which direction to look.

"Your section started here," my father points out. "That was the house, right there."

There's not much left. A hollow marking the site of the Bishop shanty. A grassy dip in the prairie, and the grass going on from there. On and on.

Gertie mumbles something, then walks out, parting the seed heads of green-needle prairie grass with a swish of her polyester pants. She stands, looking at the sea of grass, the swell of hill and sweet green valley below. She wears thick brown panty hose under her pink-edged Nike tennies. Her eyes have a sort of misted yearning for heat and cracked earth. She leans into the raw blade of a prairie wind that rises over the hill where her mother used to live.

After a little while, I walk up to her and my father stays by the truck, leaning on one cane. She tells me about a shanty that is no longer there, that she never saw but begged to hear about in bedtime stories.

"My mother hardly ever talked about it. She hated it here," Gertie explains. "There wasn't much to it. Not much more than there is now." Then she describes a tiny tar-papered shack with a dirt yard and a tin washtub, a wooden chair set out front because there were no windows to see the sunset from inside. Her mother sat out front at sunset, a younger version of Gertie, fair and freckled and sad, growing calluses and a heart full of prairie lonely.

Gertie tells about how her mother lived alone in the six-by-ten claim shack half the year while her husband worked in Murdo, twenty miles away. Pioneer women learned about silence this way, and some went crazy from it. The law said you had to live on the land to stake your claim. There were no crops or cattle to sell for the first year or two, so men got jobs in town while their wives sat in front of their claim shack's wood and tar-paper door, in polished chairs brought from far away, and listened to the cries of coyotes in the night. Gertie's brother was born in a neighbor's house, and then her mother was driven straight back to the one-room shanty, the baby in a basket at her feet.

"Once she told me why she hated snakes so much," Gertie says, almost in a whisper. "She came in from outside to see a rattlesnake coiled in the middle of the floor. A rattlesnake! Can you imagine?"

I could. The snake curled in the center of the room, unavoidable, like a round, gray rug. The baby sleeping just beyond, under a quilt Gertie's mother had carried six hundred miles. How she picked up the rattlesnake with the laundry basket because she had to get that buzzing out of her house. That coiled death. I could picture it, all right.

"I am the answer to my mother's prayers," Gertie says after a long silence. "She prayed that her next child would never see this place."

Gertie was born in Des Moines. It was a booming town then, with neat white wooden houses and trimmed grass in every yard. There were no rattlesnakes. No endless, scratching wind. There were windows in those wooden walls. And from inside the Iowa house, all sunsets looked the same.

"But look at me now," Gertie says, turning to me. One strand of thin, white hair blows across her face and she brushes it away. "Here I am."

Gertie grew up missing a place she never knew. It's all there in her eyes. The empty space and sky, hard brown stretches of prairie grass burned by an endless sun.

What will be there to read in my eyes when I am an old woman, returning to the places I have loved? Perhaps I will never leave. Perhaps I will leave and be forever returning, forever drawn back home.

I have visited Bangkok and Budapest, London, Jakarta, Cairo. I love threading through the market stalls of a crowded *souq,* pressing myself inside a crowded bus and letting it take me where it will. I never tire of watching people—there are so many faces, each one a story.

But in the end, I return here, to the prairie. Cities

fascinate but drain me. I find them alike in this way. Early in the morning, I listen to the sound of cars and people on their way to work and children crying. Trains grumble in the night, heading for someplace far away.

There is a time in my travels, in the middle of the night, when I wake and search for silence, seeking room to breathe. Perhaps the moon has risen outside my window. I know it is time to come home to the circle that is the sun's path and the horizon's edge, that gives shape to life and draws me toward my death. Come spring, I return to the wind and grass and shadowed Vs of pelicans. To my silence and open spaces.

WHAT WE LOSE

Three coyotes, twenty-two prairie dogs, a cottontail, and
a rattlesnake one day. Reload. A bag of puppies, the three-
legged blue heeler, and a mud nest of wasps another. The
coyotes we skin; the carcasses float down the White River
at dusk, tumble naked as day-old babies. The heeler is led
out behind the barn, through gates her musty old eyes once
guarded, and shot.

In that gunshot there is deafening, thunderous silence.
Something is lost.

TRAPPING BOBCATS

Before I was born, my father hunted bobcats for their skins.
He walked the river bottoms without a limp then, shouldered
his rifle the way a young ox takes the yoke.

When I am six, I watch my father shoot two trapped
bobcats in a crackling, ten-minute home movie. His hair is
thick and combed to a swoop over his left eye, belt cinched

tightly around his squat, thick-muscled frame. He shouts, "Are you getting this?" And I'm watching, that first time, without covering my eyes.

I remember the cat on the left, not much bigger than a mouse-fed tabby, a beautiful nutmeg brown and speckly cream, strung to a cottonwood trunk and pacing, writhing from a chain attached to her left paw. The bigger cat, silvery, with wide, white-ruffed cheeks like a lion, sits hunched on the log, waiting.

I don't remember the shot that kills the brown cat. She stops dancing and pulling suddenly, then droops from the log to hang by one narrow leg.

The second shot takes longer, and I remember waiting for it, flinching. The camera moves in closer to the big cat. His silvery face is balled in a snarl, then it smooths, and his eyes are slanting and yellow and sadder than anything I have seen before. He is waiting with a cat's thoughtful patience, and he is crying, or I am. I'm not sure.

I hear the shot from off camera, and like air whooshing from a balloon, the cat's beautiful face crumples. He deflates slowly, and dims somehow, until he is lying, curled tight on the trap like an old fur rug, and the sadness is gone from his eyes.

Each time I see the movie I hold my breath, hoping my dad misses, but he never does. As the flickering film replays in my mind I still hope, sometimes, but he never does.

He stopped showing the film years ago, and never really enjoyed watching it himself, I think. But I remember when he still showed it, and the look on the hunters' faces who stopped by to watch—back when I am small and curled in a rocking chair by the fire, and the movie is crackling and I am hoping, please, please miss, and he doesn't. Those hunters hungrily watch the cats die, suck coffee from hot blue cups, eat Mom's carrot cake in gulping bites, then lick their callused brown fingers.

Afterward they pet the big, dead cat that hangs on the wall behind our couch. With sparkling glass eyes and silver-spangle coat blending to cream at the belly, mouth open in a tongue-curling snarl, it is a magnet for children and hunters. Over the years, they stroke black tufts from the ears, pull charcoal hairs from the tip of the tail until bare, dry skin shines through.

"Beautiful," they say wistfully, wiping crumbs into the fur, wishing that bobcats weren't so rare now, wishing they'd see one, too, in the empty, purple black shadows of willow and buckbrush along the river.

No one sees them anymore, except maybe my dad on his walks by the river. He has grown old suddenly, and at seventy no longer hunts or wishes people to hunt on his land. In winter he dumps round bales of alfalfa for the deer and spills oats from the auger, on purpose, for wild turkeys.

He walks with Sheba, our woolly old malamute, both of them stooped and slow. Limping over uncombed tangles of brush and prairie grass and fallen cottonwood limbs, he is armed with binoculars and a cane, and he stumbles, sometimes on his good leg, sometimes on the one made of steel. He's looking for arrowheads, or something forgotten he's lost, and if he does see a bobcat on those long, lonely walks, he doesn't say.

SAVING SWALLOWS

One day many years ago, when I was still too small to reach the cupboard without a chair, I saw a swallow fly into our garage. I remember standing in the doorway watching her dive and swoop, batter her narrow wings on the concrete walls. She seemed frantic, unsure of what was solid and what was not. She skittered across the far wall, then fluttered straight for me. She hit the front of my T-shirt, hard, and clung. Too surprised to move, I stared down into her round, berry black eyes.

I reached up to cover her with one palm and still she clung. Now I could feel her heart beating, and her body shivered with the force of it. I walked outside and lifted her clear of my chest, up toward the sun. When I opened my fist, she scrabbled for an instant, dipping her blue-black head to look around, and I thought she might stay. But then she flew, with liquid strokes more graceful than any bird I'd seen before. I watched until my eyes burned and swam from looking at the sun, and by then she was just a dot that faded into blue.

After that I more closely watched the birds that visited our ranch. Robins, tiny yellow finches, bluebirds, meadowlarks and brash redheaded woodpeckers. I plotted ways to catch them, feed them, watch them. I learned their songs and whistles and answered when they called, mourned when I found the scattered beak and feathers of a sparrow killed by barn cats.

Since then I have fed a baby grackle that fell from his nest, freed a red-winged blackbird from a tangle of old screening, and caught a sparrow in my hair. Each time I open my palm, watch eager wings take flight, I can't help staring up until all the world is sky. I am not always kind, not always careful of the animals whose path I cross, but when I feel the tiny strength of a desperate bird, I try hard to remember that first swallow. I thank her for the gift of her heart beating hot inside my palm, for teaching me the beauty of life trembling in so fragile a shell.

CALVING HEIFERS IN A MARCH BLIZZARD

I grow numb. Not from the cold so much as from the sight of the dead baby calves that litter the barnyard. Each night I step over a tiny red white-faced heifer on the way to the gate. She was born dead, frozen to the ground where we threw her. Two black calves lie stiff as fence posts in the bed of the yellow Dodge; a chocolate bull calf, too broad through shoulder and hip for his mother to deliver, is laid out by the shop like a frozen steak for the dogs to gnaw.

I keep meaning to throw them all in the back of the Dodge and dump their hard little bodies onto the growing heap of calves down by the southern curve of the river. I'll do it tomorrow. Or maybe the next day, when I have a few more to add.

It's not usually so bad. This spring of 1994, blizzards
have hit one after another, snow thawing into mucky puddles
that freeze and thaw again, spread to brown lakes with the
next storm. Usually my dad has two hired men who alternate night duty during calving season. This year our foreman, Jim, quit in February, leaving our new foreman, Greg,
who is a stranger to South Dakota and the ranching life,
his wife, Deanna, and me, the rancher's daughter just out
of college, to calve out the heifers. In a blizzard. I have
learned about the signs of impending birth in heifers, the
way a vulva slackens and gapes just before labor begins. I
have learned to cut one black heifer from sixty and drive
her into a barn she had no intention of entering. I have
learned to slam the headgate shut on a wild heifer, grease
my cupped hand and naked arm with Betadyne solution
and lubricant before reaching in to check her cervix. But
mostly I have walked through endless pen slop, found calves
dying in the ice-skimmed snow between my hourly night-
time checks. This reality has nothing to do with the herd
health classes I aced in college. This experience has everything to do with death and the hundreds of different ways
a heart can freeze.

Nights run into days and again into nights, every hour
the same except for the wet of scorched coffee and birth
water. I was supposed to be good at this. My father brags
about my way with animals, my dedication to caring for
sick foals, my soft heart toward any creature in pain. He
hasn't seen me kick the poor dumb calves for dying, or

throw their lifeless bodies into the truck a little harder than I have to. It's not that I don't care, but that I can't. Death overwhelms.

Tonight it is my turn to check the heifers, spare Greg the few hours he'll sleep until feeding begins just after dawn. The white-faced heifer staring at me from the labor pen of the tilting, red barn won't wait till dawn to calve. She's been laboring since ten o'clock, and it's two now. Time to give her a hand.

Outside I hear the wind pick up, dash pellets of ice against the ancient wallboards. I pray no other heifers will choose tonight to calve.

I chase the black white-faced heifer into the headgate as gently as I can, but I am not really gentle. She wouldn't move if I were. She struggles briefly, breath rustling through her open mouth, brown eyes rolled to white. She doesn't understand. I am washing down, scrubbing Betadyne in an orange smear nearly to my shoulder when she moans through her tongue with the next contraction. Her breath comes quickly, hanging in clouds above her nostrils. She moans again, back humping up this time to push.

I cup my hand, slide my fingers past her vulva, into the heat of her vagina. She clenches down on me in a hot fist, and I move no farther until she relaxes. I thrust farther inside, up past my elbow before the next contraction, then wait. Grope, wait, grope, wait. Everything feels the same in there: wet, tense, slick. I shift positions, tilt downward, toward the cervix, wonder if I'm helping things at all.

Then I feel the calf, catch the slick rod of a foreleg for an instant before it slips away. Wait, grope. Feel a hoof brush my wrist—a soft, porous hoof, pointing down, as it should.

The calf should be pointing out, toward the vulva with his nose resting on his outstretched forelegs. This time something feels wrong. Both forelegs are there, pointing down, but there's no nose. The heifer shivers, mouth-open groan with the next push. I will my arm to relax, wait through the contraction, then slide my cupped hand up the slick little leg. No nose. Farther, and I find the nose pushed down, caught on the rim of the heifer's pelvis.

The calf moves a little with the next push, wet, moth-like flutterings under my hand. This is one I can save, and I will. I push the stiff front legs back toward the cervix, back against nature, hoping to realign the calf's head between his front legs. The cow doesn't help, resists in the way that is known to her. She pushes harder. Pushes her calf's skull deep into her pelvis's bony pocket. There is no way out for the calf in this position.

I push harder, too, waiting for another break between contractions to wrestle the heavy calf farther back into his mother's womb. Finally feel the snot-slick ball of forehead tucked deep between his knees. I slide my palm down the curve of his nose, insert two fingers into his spongy mouth. He holds my fingers with his unborn tongue, tasting blood and air and life. The next contraction nearly breaks my arm and I groan with the cow. There is no feeling so alone and yet so entwined with another life as assisting a birth. I am up to my armpits in the creation of life. . . . I feel three heart-beats pulse as one.

"Hold on, mother," I say to the heifer. "We're almost there." She seems to hear me, breathes out in short little gasps, prepares to push again.

The calf still clamps my fingers in his mouth, tight up to his hungry pad of gums. I push backward again on his eager front legs, hard this time, then pull his head up by the gums to lay between them. Yes! He is outside his mother in under a minute, bleeding gently from the torn umbilical, sneezing straw tickles from his wide, wet nostrils. The heifer rests, uncaring, as I string the black bull calf upside down from one hind foot to weigh him. He protests, bawling through his birth-wet mouth. His mother hears this, finally, and stumbles up to take a look. Wondering, snuffling mother love.

I watch for a while, marvel with his mother at curious brown eyes fringed with thick black lashes, at tottering legs unfolded and propped up, one in each corner. The heifer noses her baby, then jumps when he falls back into the straw. I laugh, rinse my puckered arms in rust-flecked well water, then snug back into my coat. The calf is on his feet again, and this time open mouth and curling baby tongue connect with teat, and all is well. I'll check them again at three-thirty, but right now I want to go back to sleep. Dream for an hour of life, rather than death.

Outside, wind dries the sweat from my face, sleet tickles through my woolen scarf. I pull open the barnyard gate, whump it closed, and begin a boot-clumping run for the house. The cold whistles through and around me, scorching my cheeks and the back of my throat. I laugh into the wind, and I am not numb.

BRANDING

Like a carnival of pain repeated every June, the stands are set and cattle are herded in for miles for the branding. Ranch cowboys unstring lariats, set up roaring propane tanks and fire pits, then chase 550 black cows and calves into corrals, a circus tent of sorts, and shut the gate.

I am helping because this is the way it is done. The calves must be marked with a brand to prevent theft, vaccinated against sickness, dehorned, and castrated. This is the cruel truth and, like it or not, I am helping.

When the branding irons are scorching hot—the lazy P, reclining E, and upright J all braided in a glowing fist—the day begins. Ordered chaos: loose blue heelers, Aussies, and Border collies snapping and barking through the fence; calves dragged from the milling pen by one or both hind legs, bawling, to the fire; young men and women crouching at heads and tails, pulling, wrassling grimly; the smell of burning hair and flesh, sharp twang of antiseptic sloshing from the castrating bucket along with blue water, knives, and nuts.

I'm standing at the gate, splattered with muck, my left side tingling warmly from the branding fire, holding vaccine guns filled with penicillin and blackleg antitoxin in my right hand, an implant gun filled with growth hormone for the steers in my left.

I helped these calves make it through the spring blizzards. Many of them I ear-tagged at birth, petting and scratching and gentling them in the front pen for a week before they were allowed out to pasture. Now they have forgotten all that. Strong and wide-eyed with excitement, they watch with confidence as pen mates are tangled, flipped, and dragged brawling from the pen. Every one still grunts and screams when it is his turn, surprised to feel the touch of rope on his own hocks.

I know that eventually all these slick new steers, and half the heifers, will funnel off our land into belching semis and down ramps into concrete feedlots. The gluttony of grain and sour-sweet silage, the stunner buzzing at the end of one more alley, then nothing. It seems a painless way to die compared to a frozen spring's starvation or sickness's staggering uncertainty. But this uncomprehending pain, this bleeding of uncertainty into simple eyes, is hard to watch.

I hope I will never get so numb that the brandings, the hunting of coyotes from the cabs of pickup trucks, the callous infliction of pain will mean nothing to me. It must mean something. I must make it mean something.

I still picture the youngest son of a neighboring rancher tossing field mice, one by one, into the branding fire. The image is as clear today as when I caught him, five years ago, swinging them by the tail from a grain bucket into the pit. He was smiling, eyes lit with laughter.

I stood dumbly, mouth open, watching mouse-shaped flames writhe and squeak and burst in the fire, tasting the oily, screaming stench. And then I pushed him backward, bucket flopping over his head.

"Never do that again," I hissed, surprised by the ash and blood I tasted on my tongue.

He sprawled in the dust on the seat of his Wranglers, blinked up at me in silence. He said nothing, then or afterward—just wiped the dust off his jeans and walked away.

I used to think this boy was the sweetest of all his brothers, all freckles, soft brown eyes and timid, tiptoe smile. Five years later, he still smiles that way, and his teenage voice is soft as feather down, but I have to look twice now to find his eyes, the curve of his smile. They seem misplaced somehow, as if part of his face got wet and washed away. And I try, each time I see him, to piece it back together.

AT THE CHICKEN RANCH

We all get a chance, some time or another, to look our ideals straight in the eye. Find out, when something is truly at stake, if we will stand up for what we believe or just look away.

I get my chance during my fourth year of college. Each morning I wriggle into old jeans and tight, faded sweatshirts, stuff M&M's, maybe Tampax, into my pockets, and drive to work. My work clothes all smell of damp, musty feathers, tarry smears of shit, hot-greased bodies, blood. Wash after

144

wash, they smell the same. I drive twenty-three miles with these clothes for company, and even on the coldest mornings, I drive with both windows cranked halfway down.

From the road, the chicken ranch looks fresh and inviting: twelve long, green-and-white metal buildings, tubs of white plastic geraniums in front of each one, sidewalks swept smooth. It is unwelcoming as hell, though, once onto the driveway, with signs every ten feet proclaiming NO TRESPASSING, and DISEASE RESEARCH FACILITY, DO NOT ENTER.

Inside the chain-link fence live nine thousand chickens, a few hundred turkeys, and six pale, full-time research assistants. I work part time, spend twenty-five hours a week in generic white overalls, a face mask, and blue surgical booties; earn seven dollars an hour feeding, watering, weighing, starving, and eviscerating chickens. I am not always sure I can finish a day of work, finish causing the death and endless suffering that earns my keep. But I have to eat and, as a rancher's daughter, figure I must be able to slaughter chickens. They're only chickens, I tell myself.

Marty, my supervisor, lists today's projects as I squeeze into overalls. I sit on the floor to dress, tangling as usual my ragged tennies in the stretchy white overall legs. Marty wears creased black jeans under his knee-length lab coat and a button, pinned as usual to his left lapel, featuring a yellow chicken, eyes bulging, squawking "Eat Beef!"

"Twelve-A today, lucky girl," he says, checking me off his list. "Weighing Tyson-study 1242, changing feed and water, and banding," he looks down at me, eyes glittering. "No chicken holocaust today." Laughs.

My squeamishness is common knowledge and sometimes gets me the head-twisting, gut-pulling jobs, just to provide laughs for others. But I am growing accustomed to death; it becomes easy too quickly here.

I walk to Twelve-A slowly, taking deep breaths of fresh air, as if to store it, before I get there. Each house looks exactly the same and is divided into twenty-five pens of thirty birds each. Only the size of the chickens varies from house to house. The ninety-degree temperature, dim lights, and moist sawdust bedding never change. Entering any one of them is like sticking my head in a gas oven: I unlock the door and expect to smell sweat and roasting hair. At the end of the day my mouth and lungs will clog with chicken: the powdered shit, tiny feather fronds. I'll cough into the night.

All that aside, today's job is not too bad. I weigh chicks, drop them on the scale, then cup my palm weightlessly over their yellow fuzz, over laughing, button-bead eyes. I hold their hot, breath-filled little bodies inside my fist, trying not to think of swallows fluttering toward the sky. I count backward from decimal points, rounding carefully, then record slowly, ink drying before I finish the number. I must concentrate. Mistakes could affect test results and are not forgiven here.

Good days, like this one, involve unboxing and weighing new chicks, feeding, watering, and banding. Any days requiring processings, bleedings, or lesion examinations are bad. Of course "bad" is relative and applies to my feelings about the day's work. The end result for the chickens is always the same—a little more or less suffering, a longer lifespan here or there, but essentially the same. Their lives are rounded to the nearest milligram, their deaths recorded in neat black ink. They die one awful way or another and then are thrown into the trash.

I find this waste of life bothers me less and less the longer I work here. I don't think about it. When I wake up in the morning to dress for work, I find I can't remember my dreams.

"Processing" mornings begin at six. We crate the blue bands, or odd numbers, or even entire pens of thirty.

"Hurry up with those blues," Marty snaps, always grouchy when processing, nagging at too slow or too fast crating or sloppy bird handling, which may break wings or bruise thighs.

I am barely awake and already dripping sweat, mouse-colored hair blond from the dust. Charlotte's shoulder-length hair is blond, too, and she coughs into the crook of her arm as we stack crates in pods of six at one end of the processing truck. We leave the chickens to huddle, breast feathers fluffed, to wait their turn.

The chickens are stuffed headfirst, upside down, into metal funnels—calming and relaxing, oddly enough, to the chicken—until their heads are cut off and the flutter-ing begins. In six minutes they emerge through a win-dow at the other end, headless, gutless, featherless. They plunge neck first into ice water to cool for forty minutes, then into yellow trash cans lined with ice, leg bands still firmly attached to stiff yellow legs. They move on to chill weights—weights taken after the hot carcasses have cooled to just above freezing—deboning, and finally breast weights.

Afterward, carcasses are tossed into scoop tractor buckets and dumped in a deep metal trash bin. In a few days the stench will thicken to gravy, and Marty will joke about tossing one or another of the women into the "birdie bin."

At least bleedings are quick. On this bleeding day, Tara and I are chosen to select birds randomly. She hunches into a pen across the aisle from me, all 6'3" of her bent double. She, too, used to be sensitive about the killing. A "bleeding heart" as Marty would cackle, the joke sick and appropriate today.

But Tara is quick and effective now. She barely seems to pause in each pen before clanging the door shut and moving on to the next.

My method is less efficient and involves closing my eyes and groping for two fuzzy chicks out of thirty, not looking in case I can't bear to choose, dropping them scrabbling into a cardboard box, and moving to the next pen.

When we're done selecting, it's time to bleed the chicks. I hand a live chick to Tara and try not to watch her palm it, its belly up, legs poking and bobbing like an infant undiapered, ease a needle long as my thumb into its heart, then pull the syringe.

Blood collects and pools—blood from two chicks fills one tiny glass vial. Some chicks survive, but most die slowly, blinking groggily, staggering in crooked circles around the bottom of the trash crate.

"Lesion" days are among the worst of the bad. The smell

of these chickens is ripe, rotten, overpowering even to the most experienced researchers. The chickens are half-grown, vulturelike with their motley, stub-feathered wings and pink, irritated skin around neck, belly, and anus. They live in steel-mesh cages stacked like rabbit hutches, ten chickens crowded into each tiny pen.

The results of lesion studies are a surprise, both for birds and researchers. Three color groups out of six are eating varying amounts of poison, parasites, or viruses with their corn. Nobody knows which chickens until the day the birds are dissected and examined. But we have our guesses.

"I think it's silver this time," Charlotte says, reaching in to a pen of silver-banded males. "I mean look at this." She holds up a dead chicken by one silver-banded foot, its feathers rotting in clumps, its skin purplish.

"Orange. Definitely," Marty says from three pens down. The chicken he is strangling makes retching noises, then flutters, neck flopping. Marty drops it into a crate with other dead and dying chickens. The next three he grabs are already limp, slide boneless from the mesh pen into the crate.

It takes a little while for the chickens' bodies to catch up to the fact that they are brain-dead. I hunch over the writhing crate, try to pin the dead chickens on their backs, distended bellies up so no blood will pool in their intestines. This is no easy task. Ten pigeon-sized birds flop and dance, finally quiet, then one quivers into another's belly and the crate jerks to life again.

Marty is crooning to the birds in the next cage. "How much is that chiiii-cken in the window?" he sings, off tune.

He twists a little too hard, and blood mists from the neck of a blue-banded female.

"Dammit," he sings, not missing a beat. "The o-o-ne without any head," and drops it, along with the separated head, into the crate. I elbow that one off to the side for later realignment, knowing the study requires an entire carcass, while keeping my forearm pressed into nine other bellies.

When all the birds are dead and lined up in order, I snap on rubber gloves and lay butcher paper out on the counters. We work in assembly-line silence: Charlotte and I at the far end, snipping open bellies with blue-handled scissors, anus to breastbone; Marty and Tara in the middle, pulling muddled pools of intestines onto the paper, arranging the ropy, purple strands carefully; the doctor at the end of the line, slicing open long tubes of gut with his shiny brass scissors, examining the mucous lining for holes. Lesions.

The smell of living rot, of feces and half-digested yellow corn gruel, clings to my fingernails, my hair for days.

The worst days, though, are when studies are canceled. The studies in which too few chicks, day-old from the hatchery, survive their trip, or the rare times a sponsor pulls out at the last minute, leaving hundreds of useless chicks peeping happily from under heat lamps and around feed trays.

No chicks leave the premises once delivered, no matter how healthy or untouched. This time forty chicks died on the van ride home from the airport, leaving only three hundred thirty alive . . . not enough to finish the study. Linda and I are stuck with the cancellation, the clean up.

"Ready for this?" Linda asks. "The carbon monoxide pump is still down. We'll have to do this by hand." She is leaning on a hard, wooden table, bony, awkward arms crossed over her chest. Linda is next in command under Marty, reports directly to the owner. I have to be ready.

"Let's get it over with," she continues, and turns to the first box of chicks. Linda's hands are soft and practiced. She shows me how to palm the chick, fuzzy, dandelion head pointed down, throat stretched against the edge of the table, then push with the heel of my hand, hard, into the table. Linda shows me again and again, her wrist snapping effortlessly, cusped yellow shapes dipping and soaring. The trash can is filling with chicks, a soft, buttery mound.

My hands shake. I swallow, my mouth dry and burning. I close my eyes and pick a chick from the downy mass.

Not looking is the key. I find the edge of the table with my fingertips, slide the chick along the tabletop, position, and lean. There is a popping noise, and the feeling of separation beneath my palm.

After a while a rhythm sets in, a beat I can feel through the heat of my palm. The room dances with it as the yellow trash cans fill, and the killing goes on and on and on.

"What did you do today?" my sister asks when she calls that night. I look out my window, into blackness. I pick up a magazine that came in the mail. I sit down with the phone pinched between my shoulder and ear and start looking through the pages.

"Nothing," I say. "What about you?"

～ ～ ～

The cripples are what finally get to me. It takes me a while to figure out why the perfectly healthy chicken I'd fed and watered yesterday is sprawled in the corner, looking up at me with bright, hungry eyes, unable to get up for the short walk to the feeder. Or is lying in the corner, bloody and mangled. Chickens are cruel themselves that way. They go for the eyes first in a penmate that can't move. After that, the chicken is covered with drops of blood, which are shiny, too, and his penmates peck and peck and peck.

At first I simply remove these birds or their carcasses to a crate reserved for this purpose and move on to the next pen. But I am surprised to find that most of these leg paralysis problems occur in the least invasive studies— those financed by brand-name companies, measuring the effects that feeding different varieties or amounts of corn has on breast weights.

When I ask Linda about it, she grimaces. I hand her a crate of crippled broilers from building Three-A. That study goes to processing tomorrow.

"This is one of the things I hate about the job," she says, drawing the first chicken out of the crate. She tucks the bird beneath her arm, its legs raking out at odd angles, and doubles back the neck. "You see it more and more. They're breeding broilers with breasts too heavy for their own legs."

The next bird looks up at her with bright black button eyes. His sprawl is undignified, legs poking in impossible directions beneath his massive chest. "They figure with breast weights like this, they can afford a certain percentage of loss," Linda tells me.

Linda is graceful in her killing of these big birds. She lifts each chicken from the crate and kills him in one motion. When all five have finished flopping, they lie quietly, legs outstretched, more attractive in death, somehow, than in life.

~ ~ ~

I quit the chicken ranch less than a month later. I'd like to say it was because I felt sorry for the chickens and hated my role in their sufferings. I did. I do. But that wasn't it. The reasons to quit a job like that are endless, like the fact that my work helped breed chickens too heavy to be supported by their own legs. My work helped load supermarket aisles with plastic-covered trays stuffed with impossibly meaty chicken and turkey breast for twenty-nine cents a pound.

In the end, I was exhausted by waste, by the trash cans and dumpsters filled to heaping with dead birds. By our endless, casual manipulation of life and death.

LOOKING AWAY

There is something about cruelty I have begun to understand. How nice people can inflict pain easily, without regret.

When I was very young, maybe six years old, and my sister, Brenda, was ten, we picked six puppies from a box of twelve. It was like a game. We didn't know what would happen to the rest and most likely never asked. Maybe our dog Patches knew, maybe not. She was an old-fashioned blue-heeler cross, stout and grizzled blue. Jake Holbridge's black dog Beam must have swum the river, trotted eight miles in a night and left again before we saw him. Here were twelve black-spotted puppies.

Patches watched us pick them up, one by one, all twelve. She licked the six we set back down inside the box, watched my father leave with the other six in a lumpy burlap bag. How many times that night did she nose the corners of the box, sniff the basement walls, searching for the missing six? Did she know we chose easily, for a white spot here, a belt of black around the girth? We lifted each puppy from the mess of white toenails scrabbling against the paper lining of the box; lifted them one by one to show their pink bellies and soft mother-searching faces.

The six puppies we didn't choose were drowned. My father did it himself, in the river. Later, I knew why he chose the river, which was farther away than the clear little pond where we swam. River water is heavy, thick and brown as chocolate milk. A bag sunk in river water disappears before it touches bottom. It will drift away. And the river looks as it was before.

SEARCHING FOR THE BIRD HOSPITAL

I remember the spring of '95 when blackbirds fell, fluttering from the sky, to die at my feet. Disease or the stress of endless winter tired them, and they came to me to die. That spring, winter drove back down the valley road in April, blew a sloppy blizzard kiss, and stayed another month. Calves born in the night died still wet, gumming mouthfuls of snow like milk.

Even the old bay mare in the yearling pasture, baby-sitter and peacemaker, slept one night with four black legs curled around a tree trunk, drumming wild music into bark before she dreamed. Morning came and pulled a blanket, cold and white, up over her eyes.

Everything died that spring, it seems, even the robins gathered under cedars in the front yard, starving, scattered like bloody handkerchiefs in the snow.

Seed for birds, warming newborn calves on the floorboards of the truck, penicillin, extra bales of hay: I tried it all. The only way to keep from freezing, I found, was to close my eyes and leave the faucet dripping in my heart. And still I walked through death that spring, stroked its frozen side and tossed it onto a tilting pile of bones down by the river.

I remember all this now as I read of a bird hospital in New Delhi, India, where Jain monks rescue starving pigeons, parrots, and pheasants. White-robed monks buy a pheasant from the market, feed her carefully until rusty wing tips grow flight feathers, then release her from the roof at dawn—a soul achieving flight.

The Jains practice a religion that respects all life. Monks wear filtered masks and sweep the ground ahead of them as they walk, vowing not to swallow, crush, or maim any living thing, even a single worm or timid flying gnat. Theirs is a religion in which all life is sacred.

Some of these monks even walk naked, "sky clad," they call it, before their god. I picture one of these, a naked man, sweeping the walk outside my South Dakota house.

He steps softly, never on a blade of grass and never in the mud or rain when bugs and toads must have their way. He sweeps the walk before me, brushing ants and yellow crickets from the cracks.

From him I'll learn to walk more softly, barefoot over gravel, to better feel the lives I take; so what is spilled out on the ground is never lost; so birds flock, living, at my feet.

HUNGER

I grew up knowing that all the world but Murdo, South Dakota, was going hungry tonight. Children in Africa and Southeast Asia sucked on rocks and ate thin bowls of gruel. Flies clustered in the corners of their eyes and mouths, and their bellies were swollen with hunger.

I always believed that my father was feeding those children, feeding the world, working out there on his tractor from morning until night. I watched wheat pour out of grain trucks into piles on the ground and imagined those same golden heaps arriving in Africa. I didn't know about politics and stockpiling back then, or all the different ways that children starve and people feed their selfish hungers.

My family sat down most every night to roast beef and corn on the cob, bright red molded Jell-O, homemade bread, and pitchers of milk straight from the cow. We ate from our garden and fields and herds of yearling steers. My mother ground our own wheat into course brown bread, churned pale lumps of butter from the milk my brother carried to the house twice a day in a steaming silver pail. She even spent long hours stewing cracked corn and meat broth into food for the dogs. Anything we couldn't finish was fed to the pigs and turkeys.

My mother wrestled what she could from our drought-stricken gardens. Every summer my sister and I cut up a thousand spindly beans for canning, sliced milky corn from its cob for freezing. We picked chokecherries and wild plums and buffaloberries from their prickly branches, and my mother boiled them with sugar to make jam. We canned apples and gallons of tomatoes, pickled tiny cucumbers in vinegar and dill, which soured slowly on our basement shelves.

Autumn meant digging potatoes and lugging feed sacks full of them, along with bright orange pumpkins, down into the basement. They would sit half the winter surrounded by boxes of apples and onions and squash. We ate through them all by March, then spent the spring waiting for the taste and smell of growing things. Fresh fruit was almost impossible to find in Murdo's one grocery store come winter, so once all the apples were gone we ate fruit cocktail and pineapple chunks from cans. More than anything spring meant strawberries.

We had two huge freezers, and both were always full of venison and rectangular cuts of beef wrapped in paper. There were hard little Baggies full of corn, frozen to the size and shape of fists. We stockpiled bread dough and deer jerky and countless Tupperware containers full of leftovers. Nothing was wasted.

My stomach was full, growing up, so I had to learn about hunger in different ways.

One winter, in just less than a week, a hawk killed eighteen of our new foreman and his wife's twenty chickens. Greg and Deanna's chickens were not ordinary Rockford reds or white broilers. They were beautiful birds, crowned and speckled, some with feathered legs and topknots. They were not practical birds but still busy and energetic in the way that chickens are—I loved to watch them hunt grasshoppers in summer, scramble for vegetable peels all year round. We ate their small, speckled eggs with toast for breakfast. Occasionally, Greg butchered a young rooster for Sunday dinner.

The hawk must have been hungrier than we were. We found eight carcasses the first day, spread-eagled on the tops of round bales behind the barn. One after another, the carcasses were untouched except for a bloody hole just above the breast. I was horrified.

Each day, more chickens disappeared, though we locked the coop at night. The hawk took to sitting in the highest branches of a cottonwood tree behind the barn. She was also beautiful—russet brown with a pale, speckled breast. She would take off if any of us walked too close, and I saw she had a mate who soared with her in the early afternoons. They circled high above the cottonwoods, above the White River's snaking path. They dove with lightning-strike speed to snatch up prey.

I refused to believe at first that a hawk would kill so wastefully. The chickens' bodies were never torn apart or eaten except for their livers and crops. Just flopped down on the ground or a bale of hay, limp inside their feathers. I was agonized by the loss. I learned later that the hawk was acting from instinct, storing up dense nutrients from those crops and livers, nutrients that would keep her alive if the winter turned harsh. But at the time it seemed like sheer wastefulness.

Greg ended the slaughter one morning. He simply brought his twenty-two rifle with him during chores and shot the hawk from her perch. She fell to the frozen ground and was still. The last two hens wandered out of the coop that morning. They cocked their heads to peer up into the sky, then went on their nervous way, pecking hungrily at shiny bits of ice and snow.

Where I grew up, nobody had food or land to waste. South Dakota farmers and ranchers who survived the dust bowl of the thirties understood best of anyone the mortality of earth. Its limits were burned into men's souls when pastures grew clouds of dust instead of grass, when cattle starved, chewed the bleached thighbones of other cattle in their hunger for more minerals and nutrition.

During my childhood, ranchers calculated carefully how many cattle they could run to the acre. Farmers planted cane and barley right up to the fence. We ate off the same plastic plates two weeks after a picnic—my mother washed and dried them carefully with a threadbare towel. Waste was sin.

I did my part—scraping cucumber peels and watermelon rinds into a bucket for the turkeys, cleaning my plate and eating my sandwich crusts, dropping quarters for starving children into the offering plate each Sunday.

A hawk that killed chickens and left them to rot was the unimaginable enemy. I was praying for the starving kids in Africa, not knowing that a different kind of hunger, one closer to home, had swallowed up our own continent, eaten holes into our land, into our very souls.

The early pioneers of the prairie must have given up counting doves. There were so many birds and antelope and buffalo that killing ten or twenty or a hundred at a time hardly seemed to matter. There were flocks of passenger pigeons that darkened an entire sky. The men who walked out with their guns saw that like the chest-high grass, these animals were endless. Sent like manna from God to sustain them. To fulfill a hunger that had grown as big as earth itself.

Now the tallgrass prairie of Kansas and Nebraska has been devoured by farmland and housing developments. The passenger pigeons are gone, the buffalo—once hunted nearly to extinction—are back, but confined to state parks and private ranches.

There is a gluttony peculiar to humans that, in some ways, reminds me of the greedy hawk—storing up nutrition that might be needed later, extinguishing life after life to save her own small skin.

Just last summer, I was invited to supper at Albert Baughman's house. His wife, Sarah, had grilled hamburgers and roasted ears of corn. There was a platter of sliced tomatoes, and a bowl full of sugar for sprinkling on top. Just as I remembered from my childhood, nothing was wasted.

Albert and Sarah live on the topland, just north and west of Okaton. Their house is small and square and white, planted squarely in the shadow of Albert's massive machine shop. There are neatly graveled paths leading up to grain bins, a fenced-off garden bordered by two tall rows of sweet corn. Back behind the house is a metal clothesline and nearly fifty square feet of strawberry beds.

Daums aren't often invited to a Baughman's home, or vice versa. Though the old feud is dimming, between the younger generations at least, there are still miles of misunderstanding to be unwound. So we enjoyed the novelty of eating together, talking of wheat and weather throughout supper.

Albert's barley had failed to come up after three plantings. First there was too much rain, then weevils gnawed away its roots. Now the rains had come again, making cultivation impossible, so weeds had sprouted lushly around the field. He was going out after supper to check it again. He was still hoping to have a harvest.

Sarah asked how my horses were doing, and if I was expecting any foals. She told me her canning was almost finished, and she was starting to freeze some sweet corn. I noticed she had cut her black hair so that it fanned prettily around her face. She's six foot tall to Albert's six foot eight. I'm sure she could carry two quart jars of beans in each long, red-knuckled hand.

Ken, their oldest son, thudded through the kitchen

when we were nearly finished. He was carrying a fishing pole and tackle box. He mumbled and waved as he went by—an awkward version of his father. A blue-speckled dog jumped up against the screen door, then followed him to his truck.

"Bring home some bass for tomorrow's dinner!" Albert called after him. There was the sound of an engine firing, and dust filled the narrow driveway.

"Won't be catching nothing more than bluegills in that old Thomas dam," Albert chuckled after Ken was gone.

Sarah was up again, clearing plates. She brought out homemade ice cream and strawberries. We talked about choosing colleges, and the costs of raising kids these days.

"Got everything we need right here, though," Albert said after one long silence. "Good water and land, all the garden we can grow. Can't ask for more than that."

I looked at the child's drawings pasted to the refrigerator, the 4-H ribbons and squat, golden trophies scattered around the room. Jeweled jars of tomatoes and pickles and beans lined up on the windowsill, waiting to be carried to the cellar.

Sarah held out the bowl of strawberries, asking if I wanted more.

"No thanks," I said. "I'm full."

FENCES

As a child, I had no thoughts of boundaries. I thought the prairie began and ran forever in the hills and draws of our eastern pastures. There, the horizon was a great circle made of hills that had no end. A little farther to the east, toward the great Missouri River, the prairie stopped, and the checkered gold and green of farmland began. Farther west the badlands claimed miles of bitter silt. Just south, grass dwindled to clumps in the low Nebraska sandhills. But mine was a world of prairie, of endless grass and sky.

The land had been broken up and fenced on section lines long before I was born. As a child, I barely noticed. The sky came down in a bowl around me, the loop of a giant lariat. My horse was a sorrel speck in a world of yellow-green, and I was small, insignificant. I could ride for miles and never reach the end of my father's land.

We moved the herds of cattle from pasture to pasture in the summer, every couple of weeks when it was dry, so the land was crisscrossed with old and new barbed-wire fences.

One of my jobs was to ride the fence lines, looking for wires snapped or sagging to the ground, anywhere a cow could sneak through, a horse could catch a leg and pull. I carried fencing pliers and a few wire clips in my saddlebags for emergency repairs, though any serious fencing, as we called it, would be done by Howard or another of the guys. I was more or less a scout. I rode in a happy daze, and as I got older, took a tiny radio along. I strapped it to my saddle horn and listened to the music's relentless blare. Soon I started riding by breaks in the fence, not seeing, when the radio was on. So one day I stopped carrying it, and I rode in silence. I began to notice things again.

Our land started in the White River bottom, then continued north, stretching as far as you could see on both sides of the gravel road leading to town. The pastures I knew best as a child lay east of the gravel road. Of those, the dog-town pasture was the farthest from the ranch houses and barn. It was a desert of half-chewed grass, powdered dirt, and prairie dog holes. This was the best pasture for meeting up with a rattlesnake or tiny burrowing owl, due to the prairie dogs, of course. The dog-town pasture bordered the railroad tracks, though the trains had stopped coming through years ago. The grass grew tall and wild all along those abandoned tracks, so this was a good place to see a fox or deer. Sometimes pronghorn antelope would find their way onto those tracks and panic when they saw me. They ran between Baughman's bumpy field of winter wheat on one side and our dog-town pasture fence. They scooted west, out toward the gravel road, their narrow legs pumping over trestles and ties. I wondered where they stopped.

There was CRP land along the gravel road, untouched for the whole seven years of the federal Crop Rotation Program. I knew that it was especially important to check this fence, since the government could take away its payments if the yearly inspection showed any signs of grazing. But more important, this was a stretch of prairie where I could ride through grass up to my horse's belly, find a mule-deer fawn bedded down in last year's bluestem. I must have ridden by countless deer and pheasants, never knowing.

In the middle of it all was the AI pasture, a crooked rectangle of about six hundred acres, butted up to Brost's land in the east, the beaver slide pasture with its steep shale hills to the south.

Some of our worst fences belonged to the beaver slide pasture, which ran all the way down to our valley, south and east nearly to the White River's banks. Around corner posts and gates I found awkward, handmade barbs twisted onto antique wires. These handmades were spliced into shining stretches of factory-made wire and seemed out of place.

Those fence lines were full of life. Jackrabbits always running, never looking back. A female meadowlark rising, seconds before a hoof fell on her empty bowl of a nest. A kit fox—just a glimpse of a black-tipped tail, a face sharp as a cat's, before he was gone.

One fence line clung to the very edge of a great shale cliff, overlooking the river valley below. That fence tilted in places, out into the sky. One day I saw three dark birds, big as newborn lambs, circling in the sky beyond the bluff.

The day was hot and my horse and I were both sulky, prickly with the heat and searching for some chance of shade. I took the eagles as an excuse to stop and rest awhile, left the horse down by the dam to graze while I labored up the hill, squeezing between the bottom two strands of wire. I inched on my belly right up to the crumbling edge and began to search the sky. I saw nothing but hot blue and the yellow glare of sun. There were no clouds, I was hotter than before, and the birds had disappeared.

Suddenly I remembered to look down. This shale bluff was the highest peak around. Beneath me, the valley stretched green and gold to its border of cedar-blackened hills. Just then one of the eagles reappeared, rising up on a giant wind from nowhere to look me in the eye.

It was a bald eagle, and he was so close, I could feel the tremble of air beneath his wings. The eagle's eyes were dark and bright at the same time, measuring and curious. We stayed close that way for one long moment, before the eagle dropped on a current of air and out of sight.

I couldn't move for a while after that. The air seemed almost liquid; I could have touched the thick brown river by stretching out my arm, stepped out into all that air and space, swam in it to the horizon. I stared until I saw clouds become thick and white and real and sail toward me where I lay. Suddenly, it was cooler. I watched the eagles soar below.

I haven't checked those fences, crawled out on that cliff, for years. My father sold the eastern pastures in 1994 after losing his leg to a staph infection following hip replacement surgery. I still look east as I'm driving down our gravel road, notice the new owner has stretched a brand-new, barbed-wire gate, or replaced the rusted overflow pipe on the bluegill dam. I haven't ridden out there since the sale, but I see those pastures anyway, with the sureness of hours spent on a horse, one leg cocked over the saddle horn, riding miles of fence line.

Strange cattle tear the grass from those hills now, tear it out by the roots and seem to eat the black earth, too, with their long rough tongues. I don't have to stop the car and walk out in those hills to imagine it all gone, chewed and swallowed. For the first time in my life, fences don't stretch forever, always in need of fixing; now fences make my world seem small.

～ ～ ～

I shouldn't complain about my world growing smaller. I have to remember what it must have looked like before the farming and fencing. I close my eyes and see the prairie hills running off forever toward the sun. No plots of oats or winter wheat. No fence lines, roads, or telephone poles. There are still a thousand places where I can sit my horse, looking all around, and see neither hide nor hair of civilization.

What would it have felt like to see the first fences going up, just after the turn of the century in western South Dakota, after the massacre at Wounded Knee in 1890 pushed the last Lakota Sioux onto reservations? The free-range stockmen who took over from the Indians—men like Tom Jones, who ran horses on the White River breaks before the fences came—were against the coming of the wire. They knew what the shiny new stuff would do to calves and colts: cut to the bone. The Lakota Sioux weren't asked—they watched from reservations as their land was carved up into something new.

One man, John Wesley Powell, knew before almost anyone else what breaking the South Dakota prairie into little farms would do to the land. In 1878 he proposed that lands west of the one hundredth meridian be designated arid, usable for grazing only, and that farm units start at 2,560 acres instead of the 160 the government was proposing. He also recommended that pastures not be fenced and that herds run in common.

No one listened and fifty years later, in the dust bowl of the thirties, people watched their land curl up to blacken the skies, slip sideways across roads and under fences. Fifty thousand Dakotans left their farms and fences behind between 1930 and 1940.

Fences have a certain power over men and land. They are a visible reminder of ownership. They are armed with barbs or electricity to make them bite. They control what they fence in. And there is always something, or someone, who gets fenced out.

~ ~ ~

I see a dark side to the prairie's barbed-wire fences almost every time I haul a yearling colt to be gelded or a mare for an ultrasound exam to the Kadoka vet clinic. Whenever I arrive, either Walt or Kay, the clinic's two vets, will be working on a wire-cut horse. My mare waits in the trailer and I lean up against the concrete wall across from Kay and the horse, watching. I drink three cups of lukewarm coffee from a Styrofoam cup while Kay crouches to examine the horse's hock or fetlock or, in colts, sometimes the chest and belly.

Horses that get caught or chased through barbed-wire rarely make it out unscarred. While cattle can plow through fences, lose some tufts of hair, and lumber on, horses' skin is thinner, and wire cuts deep.

This time the sorrel gelding Kay's working on kicked through a strand of fence, then sawed the inside of his hock nearly through while escaping. It looks like an old cut but a bad one. The entire hock and front cannon of his left hind is raw and pink; the skin had been neatly pulled down in a triangle and snipped off just above the fetlock. Although the center is bleeding, the edges of the wound look hard and yellow.

Kay is crouching warily, balancing on the toes of her black tennis shoes as she scrubs the wound with a scouring pad. She's tied her dark hair back in a ponytail and is biting her lip. I can tell from her expression that this wound is not healing well. Her eyes are small and dark as she flushes the loose granulation tissue out with a squirt of watered-down Betadyne. She's not even chatting with Cory, the teenage assistant holding the horse, as she normally does. She's working, ignoring Cory, who has a chain strung over the gelding's nose, and the horse is ignoring them both—isn't trying to kick or even move away. He's one of those blaze-faced sorrel ranch horses that's seen just about every-thing and learned not to wonder about things. His eyes are dull, staring at nothing in particular.

I watch closely while she bandages him: a rectangular, nonstick Telfa pad placed directly over the wound, followed by a winding length of gauze, thick sheets of cotton, and finally a red length of Vetrap.

Kay stands up and sighs. "That's it," she says to Cory. "I'll need the penicillin now."

The horse's expression hasn't changed, doesn't change as she gives him a shot in the neck. I see her pull back on the plunger to check for blood before squeezing the white liquid into his neck. The horse just stands there, blinks. I wonder if he'll ever trot out sound with that hind leg, and hope so, for his sake.

I haven't lost a horse to wire, though I've doctored enough fetlock and pastern wounds to respect the danger barbed-wire poses to horses. I keep my best mares in smooth electric wire pastures, just in case. I am trading off their freedom this way, since I can't afford to make these paddocks as full of open space as our barbed-wire pastures. But when I am tempted to turn out my best mare, Summit, and her colt, I remember Brenda's smoke-colored mare, Bonnie.

She was a graceful, wild thing, poised to run from any spook or noise, just like a deer, with a strange, blue-dun coat and wide, liquid eyes. She hobbled in from pasture one afternoon on three legs, her right front cut at the elbow, up through muscle and tendon to bone. We never found out which stretch of fence cut her.

Howard doctored her for six long weeks, but she could never swing that leg forward, and never ran again. My father was a practical man and Bonnie was sent off to market with a load of cattle. She had reached, as cowboys riding fences say, the end of the line.

It's not just horses that pay this price. I've seen the empty, flapping skin of a deer caught in the crisscrossed wires of a fence. I wonder how long she struggled, if she died of thirst or if the coyotes found her first.

Pronghorns are especially vulnerable to barbed-wire. They pelter along gravel roads or over bumpy range, chased by teenage boys in trucks or on horses. They won't jump a fence, like a mule or white-tailed deer. They just scramble through, leaving patches of hide and hollow hair. Sometimes they don't see the fence at all, and the front runners of a herd will hit the fence line hard, bounce back with wires singing. Then there is the confusion of the unseen barrier, the frantic searching for a way through unscathed.

~ ~ ~

We seemed to be up against our own fences by 1996, out of money, feed, and hope. The extra pastures my father leased up north of Murdo to replace the ones we sold were brittle by the middle of July. The hillsides were armed with sharp and leafless stalks of clover, all that a plague of grasshoppers left behind. A quarter of the calves came in for weaning half blind, with one or both eyes filmed blue from grazing in those clover spikes. Others' black coats were frosted gray from eating plants that carried poisonous levels of selenium. They had little choice.

The winter of '97 blew in as a howling thing, with blizzards living in the hills north of the horizon, cows strangling on the ice of their own breath. Cattle prices dropped to half what they were three years before. My father and I felt the shame of selling open, or nonnursing, cows at $250 each because we needed that little bit of money to buy more feed. Grasshoppers had eaten all the second-cutting alfalfa. They ate the cornfield down to naked yellow stalks, started chewing paint from fences, even reduced spiny yucca plants to soft, white cores. Finally I could imagine what the plagues of hoppers in the thirties were like—though my uncles kept telling me that nothing in my lifetime could compare.

At home, worries had been piling up for several years. The sharp taste of desperation was part of a roast of beef for dinner. Nothing was thrown away. My mother piled our used clothing in shiny black garbage bags in the basement and refused to give them away, even though none of them fit anymore. We had no money to replace the finicky water pump or the ugly green stove that shocked my mother when she stirred something with a metal spoon. The bank still required its loan payments, mostly interest, and the cattle needed to be fed, even though the hay was gone. We were trapped, pushed up against a fence.

I thought that feeling of despair must have been what the pioneers felt, and the ranchers in the Dirty Thirties. This mute terror, this clinging to the soil. The dirt here sifts through your fingers. When there is rain, the soil is slick beyond purchase. Nothing holds on to it; horses skid sideways down hills, into fences, their hooves slick gray snow-shoes of mud.

~ ~ ~

Some sunny afternoons I ride what's left of my childhood universe—it's a globe I can circle in a single day. There's the trout dam pasture, with its pond like a twin-tailed comet. The irrigation dam pasture with its sun-drenched hills and double gates up north—the gate the yearling heifers used to crash through every summer, mad to escape the valley with its biting flies. The northwest pasture with its alkaline soil and furrowed washes after a rain. And finally the railroad tracks pasture with its gentle sweep of hills leading to the flatter topland. These pastures look the same as the ones my father sold, perhaps steeper, the valleys darker, clothed with crooked cedars and patches of buckbrush. I don't know why it matters so much to me that the section lines carry someone else's name. We still have four thousand acres—miles of crested wheat grass and side oats grama, and on a good year, more than enough hillsides thick with yellow sweet clover.

But I count acres jealously now, like some women finger diamond rings. When dust blows I want to catch it all, tamp it back inside our fence lines with the heels of my boots.

Fences brought limitations to the freedom of the West. As things are now, though, we need fences. With everybody's land divided, fenced pastures are the only way to graze the remaining land in sections, so that animals are distributed evenly throughout the hills, and no one place gets over-grazed and reduced to dust.

We're stuck, literally, with the fences. The prairie is still crosshatched with loops of the stuff, abandoned after the Dirty Thirties proved 160 acre farms don't work on West River soil. Every rancher I know has yanked up and dug out and wound up and restrung miles of barbed wire. Most have some scars, and their horses certainly do. A landscape of fences is part of our horizon now.

And if we look up from fixing fence, from the bounda-ries of our land, and wonder how to make the sky look big again, it's only for a moment. Then it's back to fixing fence.

BROKEN THINGS

The summer of my father's sickness, the days were so hot, they steamed up the sky. Mornings were gray and dank, evenings angry red, and the clouds became a ceiling, reflecting back our hopes and prayers.

My sister's husband, Dan, and I ran the ranch while my father recovered from quadruple bypass surgery on his heart. There were complications, and he nearly died. Brenda and my mother stayed at the hospital, Brenda keeping my mother from despair. She shone, taking charge of the nurses and translating what the doctors said for the rest of us to understand. The hospital was a four-hour drive from the ranch, so Dan hardly saw his wife, or I, my family, all that summer.

Our conversations became more and more broken that summer, as if we were talking through mouthfuls of shattered glass. I could tell Dan was feeling trapped. An Oklahoma wheat harvester, Dan had followed Brenda to South Dakota to help run the ranch. Only it wasn't turning out the way he had imagined. He hadn't planned to be a rancher on his in-laws' land, where he was responsible for everything and nothing, where his wife made the biggest decisions and left him to farm and sweat alone one whole summer while she nursed her father. That's how he saw things. The whole gray sky was closing down on him. He'd ride off on Cisco, his favorite buckskin horse, and not come back till after dark, not wanting Brenda to come home.

I lived alone that summer, in the stifling double-wide house trailer my parents had moved into after Brenda and Dan returned to the ranch. It was just a three-mile drive— across the valley and over the beaver slide hill—from my childhood home, where Brenda and Dan were living. But it felt much farther.

I learned to combine wheat and drive the grain truck, gripping a steering wheel as big around as a truck tire, somehow managing to keep the old diesel spinning along the muddy ruts. Dan taught me to back the truck straight up to the whirring auger, tip the bed back so my load of wheat could spin out onto the ground, rattle up the auger's skinny neck, and pour into the shiny, silver bin.

Waiting for the wheat to spill and be sucked up took awhile, so we stood in the grain dust and hazy sun and watched. I was worried about my father but didn't want to think about it, so I listened instead. Dan was slow to speak with most people. Even with his wife, it seemed. But he talked to me that summer.

Dan's childhood was nothing like Brenda's and mine. His mother was an exotic dancer. A half-breed, he called her. She had given Dan his brown hair and black eyes and an angry space inside that he kept hidden. She abandoned Dan and his brother when they were six and eight, so Dan grew up in a home for boys, learned to watch for his father's visits on holidays and between bouts of drinking.

Dan's life was already broken before this awful summer of 1993. His best friend, the man who took him in at sixteen and treated him like a son, had died of a heart attack the previous summer. He went to that funeral alone and spoke of it to no one.

Not long after, his real father had also died. Dan's eyes were hard and dark when he talked about his birth father. He told me about him because I was standing there in that grain dust, or sitting beside him in the truck on a long haul to pick up yearling bulls. Or because he could see that I had secrets, too. It wasn't that he wanted to tell me, but that he had to. Sometimes I would have preferred the silence. I never told Brenda the things he told me. Now, I wish I had.

Dan claimed he felt nothing when his father died. He said his old man had called from El Paso the night before he died, knowing. Dan could think of nothing worth saying. They hung up after ten minutes, half of that time spent in silence. Dan drove down to the funeral and oversaw the arranging and dressing and combing of his father's corpse. He had taken a comb and parted his father's hair the way he liked it, and remembered turning around to joke with the funeral director about something. He was surprised when nobody laughed. He came back with his inheritance— a worthless Mexican guitar and a straight razor in a leather pouch.

I watched his eyes when he talked, when he brought a bottle of Southern Comfort to his mouth as if he could've chewed the glass with his teeth. I thought I saw clouds, moving swiftly. Trouble. A storm blowing in. And I knew that all our lives were about to break apart.

There is no such thing as a city landfill, where I live. Everything that can't be used or understood is burned. What doesn't burn is left to rot on some forgotten corner of the land. We call our corner the bone pile, a place for broken things. One Massey Ferguson tractor. Four electric waterers, rusted through, and a pile of mouse-eaten halters, frayed to strings. One pink porcelain toilet that didn't flush, and two yellow-stained sinks. One cracked curling iron with a tangled cord. Tin cans, electric skillets missing lids, nubby-headed dolls with perpetual winks.

Everything that will not burn or bury or blow away.

The heat was suffocating that day—like breathing through hot, wet wool. But in my frantic push to work, to keep my hands and thoughts busy, I had forgotten that there were bulls standing in a corral next to the barn. They needed to be out to pasture, breeding cows.

I took them myself, ramming them into the sweltering trailer with a cattle prod and my unsteady voice. I was surprised they moved away from me. I was crazy with the heat.

The truck staggered up the steep hills on the way to the pasture gate. The bulls were jostling back there, crowded into a dark place away from the sky. I pumped the gas and shifted into second to make the hill, and still the tires spun, spitting gravel back onto the trailer's nose. I was relieved to see the gate poles up ahead. The truck's engine idled loudly while I opened the gate, then roared as I pulled off into the knee-high grass.

The radiator exploded while I was unloading the bulls. It must have been boiling hot the whole time I was un-stringing the barbed-wire gate, parking the truck cockeyed so that the tailgate pointed out into the pasture. I hadn't noticed.

I heard a hissing while I was goading each bull out of the darkness of the trailer. But it was muffled by the bulls' grunting leaps to freedom. They scrabbled out into the grass with sea legs, kicking the sides of the trailer with their thick, manure-clotted hooves. The last one, a scrawny black yearling, was scrambling, undecided, when the radiator ex-ploded. He spooked, snaking a single hind leg out at me as he jumped. It was a pathetic kick, mostly flinging shit onto the trailer door and my jeans. I left the door swinging and ran to the front of the truck.

Steam was everywhere, running up into the sky in puls-ing, white streams. The hood had blown straight up and stayed there. The radiator was split down the middle.

I stood with my hands dangling, useless. There was nothing I could do. The bulls rumbled off in a pack, the yearling trailing behind, disgruntled. They were heading for a tight black shadow on the dike of a distant dam. I could barely see that it was a cluster of cows, bunched up against the heat, but the bulls knew.

The truck continued leaking steam, hissing and moaning through its open wound. I began to walk the four miles home.

The road was hot to the touch. Each rock seemed to hold the fierceness of the sun inside itself. I could feel the heat through the worn-out soles of my boots. My neck and forearms and the top of my head, even under my hat, prickled with it.

I was looking down, away from the glare, and didn't see the snake until my boot was coming down on it. The snake had dusty diamonds on its back. Its head was a perfect wedge; I saw black, unmoving eyes. Somehow it slid away before my boot touched the ground. It disappeared into the tall grass along the road before any part of me woke enough to shout, "Danger! Rattlesnake!"

I felt something, though, as I watched the dusty rattles slew off between the stalks of grass. I stopped and looked at the S-shaped curves the snake had left in the dust, the print of my old Acme boot heel breaking its sinuous beauty. I was dumb with heat but not afraid.

When I made it home, the shade had never felt so welcoming. There was a message on the answering machine, my sister's voice, saying my father's operation had begun and was going well so far. She asked me to pray, because the doctors were holding my father's heart outside his chest this very moment. He was split open to the sky. For the first time in my life, I knew that my father's heart had stopped while mine was still beating.

How could I have forgotten? But I had, and suddenly the truck's burst radiator became huge, meaningful. The snake I had not stepped on was God's unwilling messenger.

The phone rang while I pondered this. Frantic with relief, my sister asked where I'd been and told me my father was alive, somehow all at the same time. She asked for Dan.

I knew he wasn't in the house. His truck was gone, and so he was probably combining wheat on the other side of the river, or off to Murdo for some parts and a paper-covered bottle. I didn't tell her that. We talked for a while about the bypass operation, and how one of the nerves leading to my father's diaphragm had been damaged, so he was having trouble breathing. He would have to be on a ventilator for a while.

I imagined the hollow tubes leading out of my father's mouth and nose, the smell of yellow antiseptic scrub, and cold metal bed railings. I conjured the wound in my father's chest, the leaking blood, and the misty air pumping into his lungs. I knew I should have been there. But also knew that somehow, on my long walk home, I had been.

When Dan came home that evening I was still sitting in the kitchen chair. He asked me what had happened to the truck. He had seen it parked out in the pasture. I shrugged. "Radiator blew," I said.

"Not a hose?"

I shook my head.

Dan grunted, tolerant toward me, at least, in his new and

bitter skin. He had other worries, or he would have jumped on me for overheating the truck. He rubbed his shorn head with one huge, grease-stained hand.

"Jim will tow it in tomorrow," he said. "Been about to break down for a while. We knew that."

"Almost stepped on a rattler while I was walking home. Big one, too," I told him. I wanted to shock him out of that faraway look. I wanted him to ask about my father.

Dan smiled, eyes dark and mean, then grubbed in his front pocket and held out a bloody nub of rattles, nearly as long as my little finger.

"There's your snake," he said, laughing. "I got him on the road, on my way back from town."

I looked at the rattles and then away. My sister called just then, this time talked to Dan. He sat on the sofa, holding the phone a little away from his ear, that blank stare on his face that I knew so well.

For a moment, everything was clear, the way a picture window is when it's lit up at night. I knew that Dan was leaving. My sister, the ranch, our family—it was all breaking up into pieces. All of it.

I thought about this on the way back to my parents' house. What should I tell Brenda? She had no idea Dan was unhappy. My head was spinning and empty at the same time. No words seemed to fit.

Dan and I drove to Sioux Falls on Sunday to see my father. I had four hours in the truck to prepare myself but still wasn't ready to face the hospital, a place as far away from earth and sky as anyone can get. I didn't want to see my father in a place like that.

On the way, Dan talked about the new tractor he was buying on a ten-year payment plan, the land he and Brenda were leasing for themselves up north of Murdo. He didn't seem to be able to stop talking. There was a desperate hope in every word he spoke. I wanted to believe it.

Once we got to the hospital he became silent again. We found my mother and sister in a waiting room. They were both bent over complicated cross-stitch patterns. Brenda's was barely begun.

"You made it!" Brenda said. She got up to hug Dan, and then me. She started telling us, right away, about my father's condition. Her blond hair fell across her forehead as she spoke, and she seemed to be reaching out to Dan with her blue eyes alone. I could see that he was hardly listening. I turned away.

My mother got up, and we walked across the hall to a set of swinging metal doors. A sign above the doors said CCU. Critical Care Unit. I didn't want to go in.

Brenda led the way and seemed all confidence from the way she walked. She said hello to the nurse at the desk. My mother looked small and pinched inside her bright pink sweater. Her face seemed yellowish and out of place beneath the fluorescent lights.

The CCU was a semicircle of pastel curtains. Some were open, and I saw people lying in beds surrounded by machines and monitors. These machines hummed and beeped and actually breathed for the silent people in the beds. Some monitors drew crooked lines to represent a heartbeat, the shape of a life. My father's curtain was closed, and I didn't approach it with the rest of my family. I couldn't stop seeing, noting things in my head the way a journalist jots down notes on paper. It was my way of staying apart.

I finally slipped behind the curtain, still not quite looking straight ahead. I saw a gray-faced man who could not have been my father. His eyes were closed and a thick tube snaked down his throat. His lips were dry and cracked and spread wide around the tube. The nurses had tied his hands down to the bed so he couldn't pull away his tubes and cords in the night. He thrashed feebly toward the sound of my mother's voice.

His situation didn't really hit me until I saw his clothes draped over a chair on the other side of the bed. They were the only spot of color in the room, his faded brown work pants and blue long-sleeved western shirt. His worn leather belt drooped toward the floor with its familiar old buckle— a golden agate that he'd found on the ranch, polished, and cut into a perfect O.

His clothes hung as if he'd just stepped out of them, as if he'd expected to swing his legs over the side of the bed come morning and pull them on again. The clothes lay limp and faded on the chair. This was all I could recognize of my father's life.

I don't think my father saw me that day. His eyes were confused. His chest was an angry red. The edges of the wound met crookedly, like a mouth full of broken teeth.

I felt as if his heart had been torn, then sewn back

together. I wondered if he, if any of us, would ever be the same.

The summer did not get better. The humidity continued, and even on days when it was dry enough to harvest wheat, we had to set up fans to blow excess moisture from the grain bins.

My father stayed in the hospital ninety days. The doctors cut a hole in his throat for the respirator, and he lived like that. I saw him every other week. When he wanted to talk, my sister held her finger over the hole in his throat. His voice was strange and raspy, breaking like a teenage boy's. I tried to understand what he was saying, watching his eyes for clues. He wanted to know about the wheat harvest, and if we'd turned the bulls out on time. I told him everything was fine.

On the ranch, days washed into each other. Every morning the sky broke gray and undecided. Dan's eyes were disappearing in his face. He swung wildly between hope and anger. One day he barked at Jim for driving the new John Deere too fast. The next he berated Jim for working the same field too slowly.

Once, after a rain, a semi carrying huge, toothy combine heads up to our topland field slid sideways, nearly off, the beaver slide hill. The road leading up was dirt and gravel, straight up, straight down. It was steep enough dry, but wet it turned to something like ice—slick, black gumbo. From on top it was a sheer drop to the valley floor, two hundred feet below.

It took days to pull the semi off the edge and continue

up the hill. Evenings, I rode my horse to watch the truck teeter, wheels half on ground, half hanging in the sky.

Dan left in November, when I was back in Colorado for my final semester, and my father had been home from the hospital for two months.

Brenda told no one, at first, after Dan informed her coldly during supper that he was leaving. That he no longer loved her.

She went a week like that, her husband leaving, always, but not yet gone. Later she told me it was like living with a ghost. He ate and slept on the couch and refused to answer when she talked to him, when she pleaded with him to tell her why, to give her a second chance.

When Brenda finally called, it was all I could do to keep the phone pressed to my ear.

"He's leaving me," she whispered. Her voice was smaller than I could ever remember, breaking at the edges because the words were formed from tears. "He says he doesn't l-l-love me," she said. "He never l-l-loved me."

I had waited too long to tell her what I suspected, to try to help. Brenda had always been the one in charge, knowing what to do. She had always held God and all the answers in her clear blue eyes.

Now she was lost, her marriage broken. I could have warned her. I had stayed silent too long.

I can't help but think of that summer as the beginning of the end; the summer our lives began unraveling, when it seemed there would be no one, nothing, to stitch it all back together again.

Brenda is in her second year of residency as a family practice doctor now. She has been divorced seven years and no longer sounds lost when I talk to her on the phone. I know she is stronger, more independent, building a new life for herself in Dallas, far from where we started ours. For my sister the unraveling happened quickly, tore her apart. But she came together stronger, more giving and forgiving than ever. She is following her dream, once again bright and teasing, in charge of her life, and she and her boyfriend, Mark, will soon be married.

My father recovered from his heart operation but lost his left leg to a staph infection the summer after. The rest seems inevitable now, as does any piece of history. Soon after he lost his leg, he sold nearly three-quarters of the ranch. Two years after that, cattle prices still hadn't gone up, the bank stopped lending money, the credit card debt had risen too high, and we were forced to sell the cattle and lease out the land. Many of the pastures I wandered and loved as a child have been broken up by barbed-wire fences into someone else's fields.

My father, tapping forward with both canes, takes half an hour now to walk the hundred yards to the barn. Any ruts or rocks in the road must be maneuvered slowly. I've stacked straw bales for him to sit and take a rest on before walking back to the house.

He likes to talk to the mares and foals. He leans in close

to the bars of the stalls and makes chewing noises. Sometimes the foals respond by opening and closing their mouths,
chewing air—a gesture of respect. He is delighted by this play
and encourages them to nibble on his hands and shirtsleeves.
I have worn out words asking him not to do this, telling him
it makes the colts mouthy, liable to bite fingers. I say this,
and he nods, turns to make his way back slowly to the house.
The next day he's letting colts mull and taste the collar of
his brown denim jacket and lip along the smooth length of
a crutch.

I give up and smile along. The colts will be fine. My father has moments of happiness, still, and they shine like the
glimmers of pure light before the sun sinks beneath a cloud.

There are days when I still turn around with my heart
pounding in my throat, thinking I hear Dan's voice above
the roar of the grain auger. I haven't found anyone else on
the ranch I can talk to so honestly, who understands about
desperate hope, about broken lives. I wonder where he is and
if he's happy. I wonder sometimes what Dan would say about
all these changes if he were here to see.

My parents still believe; they are sustained by faith in
the goodness of God. Their belief makes even hope seem
shallow and washed-out in comparison. I want to believe
in the wholeness of things, in a purpose, but I can't. I find
God, instead, in small moments of light and darkness, in a
shattered glass bottle lying on river sand, picking up a thousand different lights. Glass that would be no more beautiful
whole.

THE RIVER'S PATH

For most of my life I've lived next to the White River, defined my seasons and the lay of my family's land by the river's ever-changing twists and turns. The river is greedy, owning us rather than the other way around. Every spring we lose acres of bottomland field to its newest crick and curve. In fact, *National Geographic* once named the White River the world's most crooked river. I'd say fickle is more like it. The river meanders along, doubling back like an oxbow, to eat itself, moving within yards of its next curve, then moseying off again just when it might cut through. My father lost as much land as any other valley rancher, maybe more, but he was always proud that our river was famous for something, at least, and managed to tell everyone who visited about the honor.

There wasn't much else to brag about this river. The White River, true to its nature, produces the toughest, mud-diest, ugliest fish around. Back when we irrigated from the river, we'd find catfish as long as a man's leg, and stronger, sucked up through the pipes and spit out into the field. There were snapping turtles big enough to take off a man's thumb. One of my cousins once hooked an alligator gar—a strange, flat, silvery fish with wicked teeth and skin so tough my mother gave up trying to prepare the fish for supper. Still, people fish out of the river and even claim the catfish are good eating certain times of year. I stick with our dams, where I can see what strikes my line, and the bass come out tasting like fish instead of mud.

In the early spring, sometimes as soon as January, the river ice begins cracking and crumpling. For a space of several days the ranch sounds like a war zone—cracking reports like rifle shots, roarings and shatterings in the night. Sometimes the ice jams solid, refreezes, then goes out again in a flood of icy water, frozen logs, and chunks of ice as big as pickup trucks. These floods devastate the bottoms, flattening young trees and fence lines alike. Miniature icebergs litter the fields and block the back roads the rest of the winter, and come summer, crops don't grow well in the layer of sand the flood has left behind.

Often these floods uncover bones: the old bones and worn teeth from mammoths and buffalo; the more-recent bones of cattle, saddle horses, perhaps even children; the bones of anyone or thing unlucky enough to trust the river's waters and powdery banks. The White River's flat brown sandbars are deceptively smooth and firm, looking to a thirsty man on a thirsty horse like a good place to stop for a drink. Underneath that sand the water is always moving, though the term "quicksand" is deceptive, too, for the sinking happens slowly. But the river moves where it will and swallows what it wishes. We who live on its banks are only in the way.

My sister, Brenda, trusts the river more than I, though she shouldn't. She was always the one wading out to catch minnows or take a look at some bones uncovered in the far bank, or being sent across by my father or brother to fetch something on the other side.

When Brenda was eleven years old my brother David convinced her to wade across to find his model rocket, which had shot up and over the river in a streak of light, landing on the Mellette County side. David had an excuse for not making the swim—his left arm was still in a sling after he'd broken his collarbone playing basketball—though I think he would have asked Brenda to get the rocket anyway. Brenda wasn't one to turn down a challenge, so she swapped her jeans for cutoffs, found a likely stick for prodding out quicksand, and waded into chest-deep water.

"You're sure there won't be snakes?" she'd asked before stepping in. This was a strange question coming from Brenda, who had already killed a few snakes from horseback and wasn't usually afraid of such things. But she asked that day.

My brother scoffed at her. Everybody knew it was cottonmouths, not rattlers, that lived in water. This wasn't Mississippi for goodness sake! So Brenda went in.

Halfway across, she spotted the snake. It was swimming with the current, just its brown, wedge-shaped head and string of rattles poking above the water, a three-foot-long ripple in between. It was enough, though, and heading straight for Brenda.

I was a little girl, seven years old, standing on the bank next to my brother. I remember asking, "Is that a stick?" and David not answering. When Brenda waded back to shore faster than she'd gone out, with something like a rubber belt draped over her walking stick, David finally grunted and said it was a snake. I watched, wide eyed, as they killed the snake and twisted off the rattles, then threw the narrow carcass back in the river, where it went on the way it had come.

"It's all right now," David said when the dead snake was out of sight. "You can go back in."

"You go get your own stupid rocket," Brenda said, and stomped back to the house with her legs and middle coated pearly brown, looking like she'd just been dipped in chocolate milk.

Years later, when my sister was in her twenties and married to Dan, she let another man send her into the river. This time it was my father asking Brenda and Dan if they'd wade out into a channel the river was trying to break through and give it some help with shovels.

My father was philosophical about the river and its path. He figured it was moving anyway and was open to suggestions as to where it might go next. We had to try, at least, to convince it to go in the "right" direction. This time sixty acres of land had been cut off by a loop of river that was moving slowly, in the "right" direction. My father wanted to speed things up a little, so we might gain access to this land again.

Brenda had had some years to think about the wisdom of venturing into the river, but Dan seemed ready to go in, and my father reassured them.

"Safe? Sure it's safe. That's not quicksand," he said.

Armed with shovels, Brenda and Dan waded in. They were only a few feet into the thick brown water when Brenda thought she felt the sand shifting under her feet.

"I think it's quicksand, Dad!" she shouted.

"That? Quicksand? Naw, you'd know quicksand," my father said, and started on a story about an old-time cowboy whose horse had disappeared out from under him at a watering hole along the riverbank.

"If you're sure," she muttered, pressing on. Each foot made a slurping noise when she lifted it from the water, and sank eagerly when she placed it down again.

Dan, new to South Dakota and this harmless-looking, slow, and shallow river, was out ahead of his wife, thrusting his shovel into the murky channel. From Brenda's vantage point, she could see that the water was either rising at a rate of inches per minute, or Dan was sinking at the same rate.

"Dan, you're sinking," she said calmly. By this time, she noticed she was sinking, too. She lay the shovel sideways on the glistening sandbar she'd been aiming for. The sand was over her knees now.

Dan looked around, surprised. He'd been sinking so slowly he hadn't even realized he was being swallowed. The water was up to his chest.

"You think we should go back?" he asked. By this time, my father was busy poking around in the brush, looking for buffalo skulls, and hadn't noticed that his daughter and son-in-law were slowly being eaten by the river.

"Lay your shovel down and lean on it," Brenda suggested. She was having some luck with this lean-and-wallow method and had managed to turn around. Dan struggled briefly to walk normally out of the quicksand, then gave in and tried balancing on his shovel. It worked.

My father was surprised to see them out of the river so soon, covered with muck, exhausted, but with no appreciable work done on widening the channel.

"Giving up?" he asked. Brenda glared at him with ice-blue eyes.

"It was quicksand," she said. "We almost got stuck out there."

My father glanced up and down the river, then up at the sky. "Well, there's no storms coming, so you'd have made it out in time. Oh yes, you have to watch out for quicksand." And then he started telling a story about a cow he'd found buried in quicksand up to her ears, and how she'd been gentle enough to ride by the time he'd backed the tractor around and pulled her out.

~ ~ ~

My father and the river made the *Rapid City Journal* when I was twelve years old. He had devised a way to cross the river that cut down on the dangers of getting stuck, either by vehicle or horse, and avoided wear and tear on the machinery.

He had built a cable car and pulley at the point of our busiest crossing, and whirring across the roiling water in the wooden car became one of the highlights of a visit to the ranch. It wasn't as much fun for the guy who had to heave the car, hand over hand, the last few yards to the platform, but everyone admitted it was the best way to get across. The reporter took a picture of my father standing beside the car and a few of us whizzing back and forth.

Crossing the river was a necessary, constant, and changing battle. Almost every vehicle on the ranch had been through the river, maybe stuck in it, once or twice. River water dried to a film of powdered dust—hard on bearings and transmissions. One time Norman Godfry, a temporary hand, got the old yellow Caterpillar stuck in the crossing. He tried for days, unsuccessfully, to pull it out, but only managed to get another tractor stuck, and eventually, to rip the Caterpillar neatly in two.

In the winter, when it was time to bring the herd home from their fall grazing, we had to wait for the right weather, then pray the lead cows would cooperate. My father drove a tractor backward ahead of the herd, luring them with a nice green bale of alfalfa clenched in the teeth of the tractor's bucket. The cows sometimes followed hungrily, right out onto the ice where we had unrolled round bales of straw for added traction. If the ice held, and the lead cows didn't spook, the whole herd would trail across this way.

Most of the time it wasn't so easy. Some years the ice would go out early, and we'd have to drive the cows through ice-cold water, trusting our horses to dodge the floating logs and chunks of ice. Other years the cows in front would balk at the last minute, and the cowboys behind had to whip and ride to force the herd down onto the ice. Sometimes these same cows would change their minds midriver. One cow spinning around and heading back could mean the whole herd making a break for it. So, pushing and shouting, we had to keep our horses on their tails the whole way across until the last cow trotted onto solid ground. Because it was best not to ride a horse on river ice, we all hoped the cows would go across slowly so we could dismount and lead our horses behind the herd.

I never trusted the ice, no matter how deep we had chopped the water holes the day before. I walked quickly, on the toes of my boots, never looking back, giving my horse plenty of rein so at least he and I wouldn't go down together.

~ ~ ~

The White River has always had a hunger for horseflesh, it would seem. In the early days of the free range, cowboys learned the hard way how to choose crossings. Even the best cow ponies could bog down in the White River, and a cowboy was playing with fire if he whipped an unwilling colt out onto the sand. More often than not the horses knew best and would refuse to venture onto quicksand. But sometimes they seemed hypnotized by the water and would freeze in terror, or even lie down, in the middle of the river.

We nearly lost a three-year-old gelding, a leggy rose-gray named Shi, this way. Norman Godfry, who didn't have much luck with the river in general, was riding the colt that day and decided to check cows. Though it was November and the water was getting cold, Shi wasn't hot or sweaty, and Norman knew the footing was good at this crossing, so he booted him across.

They were almost to the other side when Shi stopped short, cocked his head to stare into the moving water, then slowly rolled onto his side and closed his eyes. Norman and the horse began to sink. Thinking fast, Norman jumped out of the saddle and swam with the current, holding Shi's nose out of the water until they bumped the far bank. They lay there like that for what seemed like a long time—Norman shaking from cold, the colt snorting with terror but unwilling to move, even to hold his head above water. Norman had just about reached the end of his strength, willing to let Shi float off down the river, when the colt snorted one last time, gathered his courage, and heaved himself to his feet.

My first real ranch horse, a golden palomino named Storm, was not so lucky. While I was gone on a family Christmas vacation, one of my Uncle Pete's reformed hitch-hiker convicts, a man also named Pete, whom we all called RePete to avoid confusion, decided to help out by riding on the cows across the river. Nobody had told him that a horse can't run for hours, lathered almost black with sweat, then plunge into ice-cold water. Or maybe he knew but had been drinking, and that took his sense away. Whatever the reason, the end result was the same for Storm.

Storm was a horse who loved to run. Howard often told me it was my responsibility not to let her run too far or too fast, for she was an old mare, and a gallant one, and her heart would burst before she would refuse anything I asked.

Howard never told me the details, probably figuring I wasn't old enough to know, but I can see it all clearly. Storm running, her blazed face reaching for the sky. She must have had the bit in her teeth, enjoying the run, or at least I like to think so. The water hit her hard—it must have been an incredible shock—but she kept going, only falling when she was safely up the other side. Her perfect stockinged legs crumpled, and she was dead before she touched the ground.

I cried when I found out, not so much because I missed my horse as that I couldn't bear to think about Howard having to unsaddle and unbridle her as she lay, stiff and un-moving, already beginning to freeze to the ground. Storm had always opened her mouth for me to remove the bit, then dropped her head to be scratched behind the ears. I saw her bridle hanging in the tack room afterward and cried again.

RePete apologized endlessly, but I barely heard him. I think I blamed the river instead.

MARES

Shortly after the turn of the century, just before the western Dakota plains were carved apart and fenced for settlers, Tom Jones drove a herd of horses from Colorado to South Dakota. Tom Jones was no farmer. He dreamed of running a thousand head of steers and horses on a spread of his own someday. In fact, he would settle down to run steers and horses on the cedar breaks and grassy plains between the White and Bad Rivers, and to become one of the most powerful cattlemen in the region. Then, though, he was just a hand hired to trail broom tails north and east.

The horses were a rough lot, too, mostly unbroken, a mixture of mares and geldings and proud-cut colts. Tom was paid a dollar a head to break them. These broke horses were sold to ranchers along the way for whatever they would bring, which wasn't much. The rest of the herd milled and grazed along the way. When Ann Yokley wrote about Tom Jones in her book, *Grass and Water*, the story of the first cattlemen to settle Midland, South Dakota, she said he was a horseman, first and last. He lived with those horses in every way, knew each one by its nature if not by name.

When Tom reached the prairie between the White and Bad Rivers he stopped his horse and looked around at the rolling hills and hock-high prairie grasses. I think it must have been that time of early evening when all the world glows; when after the glaring light of day, it becomes possible to dream again. He said in all his thousand miles of travel, over mountains and prairie, he had never seen such grass as this. This land, Tom Jones swore, was made for grazing horses. And he promised to come back.

As night begins to fall I like to sit out by the horse barn and watch the sun set behind the cottonwoods. The chores are done, the horses still lined up at buckets spaced along the fence, chewing thoughtfully as they gaze off into space. All is quiet except for the rattling of buckets, the occasional restless pawing from inside the barn, or the indignant squeal as one yearling shoves another from her feed.

Every evening at about this time two great horned owls begin to hoot from two dead cottonwoods just outside the horses' paddocks. They perch, two silhouettes, always in the same two trees. They make the same conversation, at the same time, every night. All that is needed are rocking chairs and a front porch to complete the image. I hoot back at them almost every night.

Dusks are best in early spring, when there is so much

to come. I watch the mares' bellies grow with a sort of awe. They are my future.

As the spring grows warmer, my hopes begin to coalesce into dreams, dreams in which I wake up knowing about a newborn foal, all bright clover smell and hot white newborn strength. I can breathe in that smell for hours after waking.

Usually these dreams aren't just of foals in general, but specific foals. Meg's colt Atlas came to me in a dream early last spring—I saw him take his first steps on pasture and, though I'd bred her to a wildly spotted pinto, saw that he was a chunky, solid bay. Meg foaled early, and with no warning, in May of 1999, while she was still on pasture. She had a solid bright bay colt.

This winter, while I was in Budapest visiting friends, I had a disturbing dream of Meg just having foaled. Her flanks were steaming, sharply concave. A tiny rope of gleaming white umbilical cord swung from her vulva, but there was no foal. I searched for hours in my dream and never found it. When I arrived home in March, Meg's belly was sucked up to her flank. She had been confirmed in foal the fall before, and by Christmas had grown a lovely rounded padding in her flank. Now she's trim and lean as her four-year-old daughter, Mina, and there's a quiet, a look of expectation missing from her eye.

The few friends I've told about these dreams are no longer skeptical. I am rarely wrong. The mares must be dreaming, too, as they knit the foals together. Sometimes

I wake with the sense that we're dreaming the foals alive, the two of us, in that very instant. Weaving bone and fuzzy coat and curled-in ears from the weightlessness of dreams.

I wonder if Tom Jones ever dreamed about the foals. The herd reached the prairie east of Rapid City in May, the time for a mare to find a silent draw or hollow, on the darkest night she could, to birth her foal. Tom Jones must have expected these foals. Few mares, even when they're fit and lean, can hide a full-term foal. With the first pangs of dawn, or over coffee, he and the other wranglers must have noticed a mare off by herself.

Newborn foals would slow the herd down, most likely starve along the way. Death of starvation or exhaustion isn't kind, and slowing down the herd was not an option either, for it was spring, the time of year for selling horses farther east.

Tom Jones loved horses. Probably dreamed horses at night. That is why he got the job of shooting all the newborn foals.

Nature is not often kind. Growing up, I watched as cows battered and killed their own calves. At the age of six, I held a pet goat poisoned by chokecherry leaves and stroked her on my lap while she died. I saw my father's hired hands shoot coyotes and badgers and broken-legged cows. I grew up in the middle of it all, this spinning cycle of birth and death, and thought I could imagine what it meant to be a horseman. But I could not imagine shooting newborn foals.

~ ~ ~

Summit already looks hugely pregnant, though she's not due until the end of June. I watch her with a worried eye, knowing she tends to foal early, sometimes very early. But so far she's still gloriously pregnant, her blood-bay coat toned with jeweled red, a hint of dapples beginning to stand out on her quarters. I smile as I watch her eat, head tipped sideways, grain spilling in a foaming mash from her flapping lips. Every year I ask the vet to file her teeth, hoping the comfort of smooth molars will convince her to eat more gracefully. But she seems to like to eat this way. Now I've noticed her three-year-old son dutifully chewing his grain with flapping lips, spilling half of every mouthful. So far, no dreams of Summit's foal.

Theory always looks her best pregnant, and she is glowing with it this spring. A golden bay with four socks and a blaze, substantially built but not tall, she can look coarse coming in from a summer at grass. But now, with her belly curving and her coat thick and glossy, she looks statuesque—"a leg in every corner," the old-timers used to say. I've dreamed of her foal already this year—a pinto filly, white, splashed with chestnut, or the lightest honey bay. This morning as I fed her, I watched her flanks jump, her belly twist and heave. I stepped inside the paddock to put my hands on her belly, felt the life inside. I wonder if Theory knows this foal already, will recognize its milky eyes and peach-fuzz muzzle, its newborn scent that will be unlike any other in her world.

Nightshade holds my eye longer than any other. She was the first filly from my favorite mare, Pine Song, and has grown up to be uncanny in her intelligence and sheer naughtiness—so far her three foals have inherited those traits as well. They look like her, too, which is a good thing. Her lines are graceful and curving, her head small and clever, like that of a keen black fox. She herds the mares in her pen away from their buckets with a single shake of her heavy black mane, then settles down to eat their share with her forelock hiding her dancing eyes. The Trakehner stallion she's bred to this year is a noble-headed bay, tall and kind, though the stallion I choose doesn't really seem to matter with Nightshade—the foal will be a naughty black or dark bay with dancing eyes and a talent for opening latches and untying lead ropes with its clever little mouth.

Busy may be carrying her final foal, and we talk of this softly in the evenings as I rub her white-streaked face. I've had to separate her from her herd, which she doesn't understand, so she can eat a processed feed instead of hay, which makes her wheeze. Busy heaves, which is a bit like having asthma. Any dust or tiny specks of mold will start her coughing, straining the muscles along her belly and flank as she forces out each breath, and will perhaps cause her to lose her foal. Once the grass comes in, Busy will be the first to move to pasture, but for now she has to wait it out alone. I explain this as I groom her, and she drops her head and sighs. When the big herd of mares gallops down into the trees, Busy stands at the end of her run and stares with longing. She is graceful in her every move, even now as she approaches seventeen. Her foals, which she and I equally adore, are long-legged, graceful things with eyes like does'. I am praying for a filly—one that will grow to replace her mother in my herd. Busy, so far, has given me no clue.

Once the grass is up, all these mares will go to pasture, and then my evenings spread to include walking over prairie to inspect udders for any sign of milk or waxing. I love walking out to check the mares. In a wet year the prairie will be alive with frogs and locusts, nighthawks and meadowlarks. The grass stretches as far as I can see; farther. The mares move across the hills, even with their pregnant bellies, with the grace of wild things.

In the midst of springtime's joy and expectation there is also fear, the knowledge of coming sorrow. I know that to love is a risky thing, whether one loves horses or humans.

My love for the mares and their coming foals has a dark center. Just as our land is far from hospitals, it is far from veterinary clinics, too. No vets make farm calls for foaling mares in this part of the state, even if something goes terribly, tragically wrong. I am afraid that one day my hands will not be enough to turn an upside-down foal, to coax a wet muzzle and two bony forelegs out of the birth canal in time. And there is so little time.

Once a mare's water breaks, the clock starts ticking. The mare has between thirty and forty minutes to birth her foal alive. This speed makes sense when you know that mares are prey animals, and birth smells like dinner to her many enemies. She wants to be on her feet again as soon as possible. But when you are behind a straining mare, looking up at the clock on the wall and waiting for two hooves and a muzzle, thirty minutes can seem impossibly short, or unbearably long.

Usually nothing goes wrong. I try to be there when my mares foal, though, just in case. This means waking up every hour, sometimes for several nights in a row, and eventually just stretching out on straw bales outside the stall. Because it doesn't take long to be too late.

Two years ago, in April of 1998, Meg foaled an immense dark brown colt. She was restless and dripping milk for three days before active labor began. I made hourly foaling checks two nights in a row; then, exhausted, I asked our foreman, Ben Seaman, to watch her for the third. I got the call at 2 A.M.

"Mare's foaling," the voice on the phone said. Ben was not one to waste words. I was instantly awake, pushing back the sheet and reaching for my boots in one movement.

I'd been worried about this mare for the last few days. Mares, unlike heifers, usually don't experience distocia, or difficulty birthing, due to the size of the foal. But my gut instinct, along with a hazy dream two months before of a mouse-colored colt with three socks and a massive, raw-boned frame, told me Meg was carrying a huge foal. She'd been bred eleven months ago to a big-boned, 17.2 hand Hanoverian stallion, and while she's not a small mare her-self at 16.3 hands and twelve hundred pounds, I was wor-ried for her. In the past, whenever my mares moved from a yellowish, waxy milk discharge to thick white colostrum, the birth wasn't far behind. But Meg had been milking nearly three days now.

When I arrived Meg was lying flat already. Her water had broken when Ben called, so I was more than ten minutes into my thirty already. I stopped to wash, slip on a glove, and slather lubricant up to my elbow before cupping my hand and reaching inside Meg. I felt a hoof immediately, and panic started tingling in my stomach. The hoof was huge—bigger than my wrist and forearm. I reached farther in and found the second hoof but no muzzle. Farther. Then back. I realized the two front feet I was feeling were flexing upward, sole to the sky. The foal was upside down.

I didn't panic, exactly. Foals often begin their descent through the birth canal upside down, twisting into the swan-dive position once the head has cleared the rim of the pelvis. But this foal's sheer size was obviously causing Meg some problems. I suspected her side-to-side contractions weren't strong enough to twist him over. I turned to Ben.

"Call Brenda and Deanna right away. I think I need some help."

By the mercy of God, or some stroke of good fortune, both my sister and my friend Deanna, whose husband, Greg, used to work for my father, were visiting for the week. While neither was a vet, at least my sister was a doctor. She'd de-livered both upside-down calves and babies—foals must be somewhere in between. In ten minutes I would know.

Meg made little progress as I waited in the shadows. I wanted to let her do this on her own, if she could. Too much interference can be as dangerous as too little, sometimes, causing damage to the mare's reproductive tract or diffi-culties bonding once the foal is on the ground.

Meg was breathing harder now, grunting with each contraction. I saw her lip curl into the straw, one slim black foreleg paw absently into the air. I looked down at my watch. Twenty-two minutes had passed. The tingling in my stomach was rising.

I heard the pickup before catching the reflection of head-lights. It took a very long time between the soft click of door and hearing Brenda whisper, "What's up?"

"The foal is huge," I whispered back. "And upside down." My voice shook. I couldn't help it. Brenda just nodded and started getting into a glove. I moved toward Meg again, talking to her softly all the time.

By now the forelegs, gleaming white inside their drape of amnion, were outside the mare, soles still pointing up. Brenda ran her hand beneath them and found the muzzle. Meg didn't seem to notice the activity around her tail. Her eyes had moved into that other place mares go inside of labor. She groaned and rolled with the next contraction. The slippery white hooves didn't move.

"Let's help her turn him," Brenda said. I'd been thinking that, too, and knelt to tear away the amnion from the two front feet.

Gently, we crossed the forelegs, careful to leave one slightly behind the other, and pulled across and down. Nothing. With each contraction we crossed and pulled, gently, always gently. From the shadows, I saw Deanna step forward and tap the face of her watch.

"When did she start?" she asked. I looked down to where

I'd buckled my watch to the belt loop of my pants. "Thirty minutes," I said. Deanna's face was grim.

Brenda and I upped the tension on the forelegs. Ben had stepped inside the stall. "He's turning," he said. We crossed and pulled one more time with Meg's next push and felt something shift. Ben was right. The foal's soles were pointing sideways now, and a white-striped muzzle lay between them.

Suddenly, with the next contraction, the foal's head was out past the ears. I stripped white sac from his eyes and ears, pressed thumb and forefinger down the length of his nose to clear his nostrils. Meg stopped to rest, then suddenly she was rolling again and Brenda had to jump back from one big black hock.

We started pulling again, over and down, one foreleg ahead of the other. But there was no give.

"Shoulders stuck," I grunted. We pulled one front foot and then the other. The colt's eyes were shut, ears plastered back along his neck. His tongue curled from his mouth, still pink, which was good.

Finally, with an effort that I could feel through the stall floor, through my grip on slippery gray-black legs, Meg pushed the foal's shoulders out onto the straw. She stopped for a moment, then groaned again. Now every minute counted double, because in this position the umbilical cord was surely pinched off on Meg's pelvic girdle, and this quivering wet foal was getting little or no oxygen.

I shifted the colt's shoulders downward, toward Meg's

hocks. She groaned and pushed, Brenda and I pulled. Nothing happened. Again. Nothing. The foal's tongue was turning blue.

"Forty minutes," someone said. I barely heard. My hands were shaking now. If the foal's hips were locked in Meg's pelvic opening, we'd have to shift him left and right, slowly, to walk him through. He was so big, though, this would take both of us.

Brenda helped pick up the colt's front end and we pulled him down and to the left with the next contraction. Then down and right. A little slip farther out. Left. Right. Nothing. Meg panted, no longer pushing. I slipped my hand in along the colt's ribs, hoping to stimulate her into pushing again. With one final grunt, Meg tried again, and all at once the whole foal was out, wet and alive and in my lap. He sneezed and took a breath, ears flopping back and down, hind feet resting inside the mare. I was panting, laughing, shaking, all at the same time. It was a colt, mousy brown with three white feet and a blaze, big as a newborn Simmental bull calf and with twice the leg. He arched his neck up against the palm of my hand as I moved away and I felt a strength that awed me. He was so beautiful. I thought I would call him Granite, for his strength and beauty and stubbornness of stone.

After a foaling it is easy to have eyes for only the foal. A new life, drawing first breath. Fear dissolves to joy.

I felt Meg's convulsions before I saw them, turned just in time to see her eyes roll back into her head. All four legs jerked, rustling straw. I ran, slow motion, to her head, and lay my hands upon her neck.

"Meg," I whispered, "come back." She shook and shook, and then I wasn't whispering anymore. "Come back!"

Somehow, I don't know how much later, the shaking stopped. Her eyes became her own again, and she lay flat in the matted straw, breathing like a horse that has won a race. I was breathing hard, too, and for a moment I couldn't see. I blinked and stepped away.

It seemed a long time before Meg tried to stand. Perhaps little Granite helped by kicking at the sack still wrapped around his hind feet. I was ready with iodine when the umbilical cord broke, and from there everything went normally, if a little slowly, for this exhausted mare and foal.

There is fear mixed with awe and expectation when I look at my pregnant mares now. I imagine the fragile strength curled inside them, the coming breath, and all that could conspire to snuff it out. In life there are few pure joys that do not come with risk, sometimes with pain. I walk the line between joy and suffering with my mares, careful to pick my way between.

~ ~ ~

In the evenings sometimes, when I am musing in the company of owls and mares and sunset, I look across the hills to the west. My gaze lingers on the cedar breaks above our valley, trying to find my way to the place between the White

River and the Bad, to the place where newborn foal bones melted into grass.

Ann Yokley wrote that Tom Jones loved horses. Knew horses. Made a living from their sweat and speed and breath. He must have loved those foals, the way any horseman would. Foals are all whiskered curiosity and wobbly-legged wonder. They snuffle toward danger the first few hours of life, blinking soft blue-tinged eyes. His would have been the toughest kind of love.

Tom Jones was probably the best shot, the surest hand with a nervous new mother. I imagine it all and wince with every imagined crack of rifle and crumpling of legs. See the mare standing, head down, over her dead foal, nuzzling hip and withers and silent, silken-whiskered muzzle. What could it have done to a horse lover to have to shoot a foal? Ten foals? Fifty, or a hundred? I hope I never have to know.

Most days, and almost every evening, I would not trade my life, this world of grass on horses' breath and the joy of coming foals, for anything. There are times, in the hours before dawn when I am sick with fear over a laboring mare or searching frantically for reasons to explain the death of a foal, however, when I think I could. I give up on joy and anguish both. But then morning comes, and another crimson evening. I watch a mare stand over her sleeping foal, run my hand along an expectant mother's flank at feeding time and feel the flutterings inside. And I am sure again.

The mares graze, peaceful, as I think on these things. They tear up grass that has been nourished by the bones of those who've gone before. In the darkest hour of the night they sleep, three legs solid and one hind cocked. The foals inside their bellies lie quiet in their warm, suspended sleep. I sleep, too. Together we dream of possibilities and the warmth of newborn breath. We dream the future into life, one foal at a time.

LAST CRANE

The last crane of the season crouches alone, in the cornfield bordering our house. I notice her on my way out to check fence: a single gray neck and sharply pointing beak swiveling first one direction, then the next. I'd heard a flock moving through the day before. I wonder if she's lost her way.

I go about my chores, looking out across the cornfield from time to time. The crane never moves. When I study her closely, through the binoculars, I see her head turn; that's all.

I think she's probably injured. I don't know why else she would crouch like that in the corn stalks—never bobbing her head down to browse for corn, never shying away as I walk between the house and barn. I think about how far she is from home.

Two things happen that day that make it hard to forget the crane. She doesn't move all afternoon as clouds shift and settle and cover the sun. I'm thinking about her while I catch the yearling and two-year-old fillies and tie them in the aisle of the barn. I wonder if I should call the game warden. Maybe keep the dog in tonight, just in case.

I'm thinking about the crane while I'm grooming the fillies and filling syringes for fall vaccinations. While I'm currying two-year-old Jewel, a black filly named Magdalene, one of the yearlings, works herself loose and starts for the door. She's just behind Jewel now, pausing to sniff inside the tack room, cocking her head a little to the side so she can drag her lead rope without stepping on it. I step back to catch her—still thinking about whether I should wait until morning to walk out and see if the crane is really hurt—and in that instant feel the breeze of Jewel's kick stir the hair alongside my ear.

I don't think anything for an instant. I turn, in impossible slow motion, and see Jewel's hoof still suspended in the air. It looks terribly close.

I yell something at Jewel that I afterward forget. All three of the fillies spook. I move slowly, careful this time, to catch Magdalene, who has skittered up against a stall door and stands there rattling breath through her nostrils. I tie her again and walk outside. The sun has come out and the day looks different somehow. I feel shaky, strange in my skin. I lecture myself on being present when I'm working with the young stock. I'd just come as close to death or brain injury as I'd like to—ever. Across the road and a hundred yards of field, the crane crouches stiffly in her chosen spot, swiveling her head to see what all the commotion might be.

When I go inside for the night the tension from the barn seems to follow me and press up against the windows, rises like steam to hang at the corners of the ceiling. My father is agitated. He looks the way he used to just before a thunderstorm, when he would pound through the house watching for hail from all our different windows, or stand outside in the rain, the screen door slamming behind him. Only this time there's no storm.

"I'm ready to go home," my father mutters, clumping toward the front door. I glance at my mother. She has a strained look around her eyes.

"Johnny, you *are* home," she says, a hand on his arm. "This is your home." My father looks around, not convinced.

"You're not fooling me," he says. "I want to go home now." His voice is strange, high and sure; not my father's voice at all.

He shuffles toward the door, toward the black outside. He will fall, and I will not be able to get him up. He will wander in darkness, looking for the place he thinks is home. I get up and reach across to lock the door. I know his fingers are too clumsy from the diabetes to turn the tiny knob. I don't know what else to do.

In the morning the crane is gone, and my father is himself again. In fact, he seems to have forgotten all about his confusion last night. He asks how the colts are doing without their dams, for it is weaning time. I am happy to tell him, and later, point out the place in the field where the crane had been.

"Coyotes must have got her," he said. "Or maybe she just flew away."

I wonder, too, and promise I will walk out to look for a sign later today. But I don't. Maybe I get busy, or maybe I just don't want to see a clutch of feathers come away from skin. I'm not sure.

Most days my father remembers who I am. He knows that the house he and my mother are living in is the one he built, the place we still call home. On the days he doesn't seem to know me, I remind him.

"I am your daughter Ann, the one who breeds horses," I say.

"Oh yes, yes, I know," he says, looking at me closely from his wheelchair. Though his eyes are dim, almost blind, I can see a certain recognition when he looks at me that way. I'm sure he does know who I am, and there is only the confusion of words between us, not of love or stories or of the soul.

My mother has come full circle, claiming her place in this family. Now she is the one to tell the stories my father is forgetting. She is the rock, the quiet savior of our family.

Now, every time I leave the ranch, I savor the drive back— seeing my parents, this land, even our hungry river, at the other end. It is my turn to hold on to the memories, to make my own.

I am weaving loss into something else. The cattle are gone, but each year I have been adding to my mare herd, breeding to better stallions, keeping my finest fillies. The coming foals are the future. In this way, with this hope, I keep returning.

It's good to know the cranes will be back next April. And the year after that. There are no sure things, but this one is pretty close. I can live with that.

ANN MARIE DAUM writes and breeds sport horses from her family's ranch, located in the White River valley of south central South Dakota. She winters in Budapest, enjoys traveling and reading in her spare time, and has loved cats, horses, and the rolling prairie hills where she lives for as long as she can remember. She wrote her first short story, about a wild horse, when she was five years old. She received a Bush Artist Fellowship in 1999.

MORE BOOKS FROM MILKWEED EDITIONS

To order books or for more information, contact Milkweed
at (800) 520-6455 or visit milkweed.org

BROWN DOG OF THE YAAK:
ESSAYS ON ART AND ACTIVISM
Rick Bass

SWIMMING WITH GIANTS:
MY ENCOUNTERS WITH WHALES, DOLPHINS, AND SEALS
Anne Collet

WRITING THE SACRED INTO THE REAL
Alison Hawthorne Deming

BOUNDARY WATERS:
THE GRACE OF THE WILD
Paul Gruchow

GRASS ROOTS:
THE UNIVERSE OF HOME
Paul Gruchow

THE NECESSITY OF EMPTY PLACES
Paul Gruchow

A SENSE OF THE MORNING:
FIELD NOTES OF A BORN OBSERVER
David Brendan Hopes

TAKING CARE:
THOUGHTS ON STORYTELLING AND BELIEF
William Kittredge

THIS INCOMPARABLE LAND:
A GUIDE TO AMERICAN NATURE WRITING
Thomas J. Lyon

A WING IN THE DOOR:
LIFE WITH A RED-TAILED HAWK
Peri Phillips McQuay

AN AMERICAN CHILD SUPREME:
THE EDUCATION OF A LIBERATION ECOLOGIST
John Nichols

THE BARN AT THE END OF THE WORLD:
THE APPRENTICESHIP OF A QUAKER, BUDDHIST SHEPHERD
Mary Rose O'Reilley

WALKING THE HIGH RIDGE:
LIFE AS FIELD TRIP
Robert Michael Pyle

ECOLOGY OF A CRACKER CHILDHOOD
Janisse Ray

THE DREAM OF THE MARSH WREN:
WRITING AS RECIPROCAL CREATION
Pattiann Rogers

THE COUNTRY OF LANGUAGE
Scott Russell Sanders

OF LANDSCAPE AND LONGING:
FINDING A HOME AT THE WATER'S EDGE
Carolyn Servid

THE BOOK OF THE TONGASS
Edited by Carolyn Servid and Donald Snow

HOMESTEAD
Annick Smith

TESTIMONY:
WRITERS OF THE WEST SPEAK ON BEHALF OF UTAH WILDERNESS
Compiled by Stephen Trimble and Terry Tempest Williams

SHAPED BY WIND AND WATER:
REFLECTIONS OF A NATURALIST
Ann Haymond Zwinger

Founded as a nonprofit organization in 1980, Milkweed Editions is an independent publisher. Our mission is to identify, nurture and publish transformative literature, and build an engaged community around it.

milkweed.org

Interior design by Dale Cooney
Typeset in Legacy n/16
by Stanton Publication Services, Inc.

Printed in the USA
CPSIA information can be obtained
at www.ICGtesting.com
JSHW021502020424
60423JS00002B/29